ROUTE 66 RAILWAY

ROUTE 66 RAILWAY

THE STORY OF ROUTE 66 AND THE SANTA FE RAILWAY IN THE AMERICAN SOUTHWEST

Elrond Lawrence

Los Angeles Railroad Heritage Foundation

To Mom and Dad, who started me on the right path . . .

and to Laura and Kat, who keep me on track.

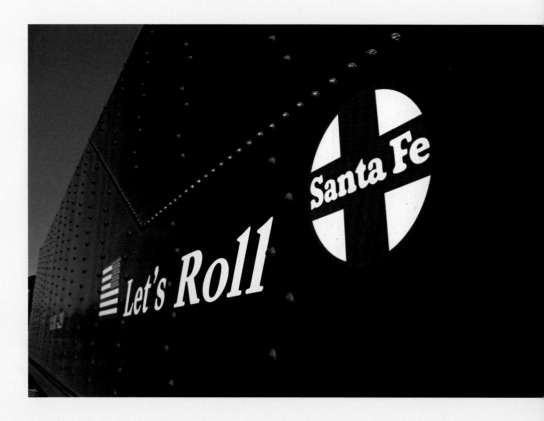

Contents

Acknowledgments

ROUTE **66** R AILWAY would not have been possible without the contributions and support of many people. Chief among them are the talented photographers who enriched this project with their wonderful images. They include Gordon Glattenberg, Stan Kistler, Howard Ande, John Sistrunk, Ted Benson, Bob Finan, Dave Ingles, Hank Graham, Kathryn Lawrence, Greg McDonnell, Richard Sugg, Tom Gildersleeve, and David Lustig. Additional vintage photographs were provided by the Palace of the Governors in Santa Fe, New Mexico; the Center for Southwest Research at the University of New Mexico; Northern Arizona University's Cline Library Archives; and Bob Moore of *Route 66 Magazine*.

Special thanks to my friend Ted Benson for his engaging foreword, and to my wife Laura Lawrence for her entertaining sidebar about neon and for compiling the book's index. John Sistrunk and Mike Martin loaned historic postcards and telegrams that add an extra dimension. David Styffe used his considerable talents to create the eye-catching maps that open and close the book. Bob Spinuzzi and Armen Alder defied spiraling gas prices to drive their beautiful Corvettes to the Mojave Desert for two memorable photographs.

I'm especially grateful to Josef Lesser and the Los Angeles Railroad Heritage Foundation. Joe "got" the concept from the beginning, and he and LARHF provided the means to realize a long-held dream. Several generous individuals helped bring this book to life, including Robert and Dennis De Pietro, Steve Garner, Ron Gustafson, Ellie and Mark Lainer, Capt. and Mrs. Walt Lester, USN Ret., Al Minturn, James E. Partridge, and Ed Romo. Thanks also to Kurt Hauser, who brought the vision to life with his clean and classy design.

Several books and magazine articles served as resources, but a special debt of inspiration is owed to Michael Wallis and his definitive book, *Route 66: The Mother Road*.

My heartfelt thanks go to family and friends for their outpouring of support. A complete list would far exceed this space, but they include my mom, Jill Lawrence, and my aunt, Maddie Chero, who have been lifetime champions. Thanks also to: Joanne Farness, David Lustig, Jim Bunte, Steve Crise, Angel Delgadillo, Shirley Burman, Martin Burwash, Steve Patterson, Joe McMillan, the Route 66 Yahoo e-group, Gary Wolfe, Robert, Stephanie and Jack Meineke, the gang at Fisher Vista, Atticus, Zoe, and Tess. Special thanks to David and Judy Alder, and to my in-laws, Jerry and Mary Mihld, for the many times that they opened their homes to a weary traveler.

Most important, this book would not exist without the love and support of Laura and Kathryn, whose patience and tireless encouragement lifted my spirits when the grind was at its worst. In addition to providing two fine images, Kat was a terrific traveling partner.

Finally, Ted and Stein opened my eyes to what was possible, and I will always be grateful.

Alray Tunnel, Cajon Pass

Ribbon of Highway, Ribbon of Steel

Saturday, September 1, 1973, had barely become the golden promise of dawn in the sky above Flagstaff, Arizona, as a '71 Ford Maverick crunched down the gravel driveway at 609 West Birch and quietly accelerated downtown in search of East Santa Fe Avenue and its namesake railroad. For Allen S. Jones, a Flagstaff resident 53 of his 72 years, the road was familiar. His arrival in Arizona's high country preceded the paving of Route 66. For his driver, the shaggy-haired twentysomething husband of Jones' first grandchild, this day would instill a fresh appreciation for a land and a railroad hitherto largely ignored. Where better to begin than that big bridge over the sinister slash in the sandstone a little northwest of Winslow?

"Canyon Diablo? That's out 66 north of Two Guns. Haven't been there in years."

Morning comes fast in the Painted Desert—the trains often come faster. The late summer sun was well above the horizon by the time Grandpa Jones and I reached the Santa Fe tracks at Canyon Diablo a few minutes past 7 A.M., intent on photographing Amtrak's eastbound *Super Chief* on the famous steel bridge. Too late—Number Four's headlight was already bearing down on us, barely allowing time to focus as a trio of gleaming new SDP40F units rocketed past the wooden signboard 312 miles west of Albuquerque, slicing the distance from New Mexico's metropolis in mile-long strips every 45 seconds.

Westbound drag freight 728 approached at a markedly slower pace a few minutes later, its eight locomotives, 68 cars, and 6,400 tons crawling to a halt at the crossover switches east of the bridge. Extended prodding behind the

Left: Santa Fe train 728, Extra 5516 West, gets underway at Canyon Diablo, Arizona, in September 1973 with 68 cars and 6,400 tons behind eight EMD and Alco diesels.

Above: Allen S. Jones passes the time at Canyon Diablo, Arizona, awaiting the passage of an eastbound Phoenix train in 1975. In the Painted Desert, there's nothing but God, sandstone, and the Santa Fe.

hood doors of the three Alco RSD15 "Alligators" behind SD45 No. 5516 eventually resulted in a smoky resumption of their climb toward the Arizona Divide west of "Flag." It was the beginning of a train-chasing day that would ultimately take us to a late lunch in Seligman and a dinner table full of conversation at 609 West Birch that evening. Neither Grandpa nor I would ever look at the Santa Fe quite the same again.

Nineteen seventy-three saw the first of three "early marriage" trips to Arizona that included driving the last great stretch of "pure" U.S. 66 between Kingman and Seligman. The classic two-lane paralleling the railroad through Peach Springs and the Aubrey Valley was a neces-

sary evil to my wife Liz, who'd grown up listening to Santa Fe whistles echoing through Flagstaff. For her unabashedly obsessed husband, Route 66 was an open book of creative possibilities.

For both of us, the highway was a means to an end, a lifeline connecting a family spread across two states—the grandmother road as well as the Mother Road. Ours was a family of Ford drivers, latter-day Joads on a pedal-to-the-metal pilgrimage of pleasure. This was no leisurely cruise with a smooth jazz soundtrack. Our "Route 66" was a rock and roll road, a passage set to the rhythm and blues of the Rolling Stones. In 1973, my appreciation of the highway itself had yet to come.

Above: Pedestrian and vehicle traffic wait on South San Francisco Street in Flagstaff, Arizona, as Amtrak's westbound *Southwest Limited* finishes its station work on an August 1975 evening.

Happily, Elrond Lawrence grew up without such cavalier attitudes when it came time to stop and smell the asphalt. For Elrond, life is a journey, not a destination.

Elrond's Route 66 may be the road less traveled, but it is also the path of least resistance—a highway where the spirits of Steinbeck and Troup trade sideways glances with passing freights, and no self-respecting traveler would even think of stopping for the night at a motel whose marquee boasts of being "away from train noise."

Elrond's Route 66 and its attendant railway is a welcome respite from an interstate world where the miles are merely measured by hours. This is a road one *chooses* to travel, a place where Needles is far from "Needless" and the quality of the drive is measured by the hours invested in places like the Jackrabbit Trading Post, Snow Cap cafe, and Wigwam Motel—a lodging famous for train noise.

More than two decades have passed since U.S. 66 was decommissioned in 1985. "Atchison" and "Topeka" have been missing from the Santa Fe Railway name since 1995, initially replaced with the title of merger partner Burlington Northern and today simply referred to as "BNSF." Through it all, the Mother Road and her Route 66 Railway remains an indelible element of the American fabric—history, myth, and manifest destiny entwined in one ribbon of highway and two ribbons of steel.

Thanks to Elrond Lawrence, it is a journey to savor again in the following pages.

TED BENSON
MODESTO, CALIFORNIA

It's 1973, and Amtrak has been in charge of passenger service across Santa Fe's Transcon for more than two years . . . but the Harvey House train board at Seligman, Arizona, has yet to acknowledge it.

Introduction

"It's not the years, honey . . . it's the mileage."

— INDIANA JONES

HERE IT IS. The words reflect a sense of optimism, of arrival. They also reflect the completion of a dream that first began in 1991.

Route 66 and the Santa Fe Railway have been part of my life for as long as I can remember. I grew up in the steel mill town of Fontana, California, just blocks away from Foothill Boulevard (a.k.a., the former 66) and Santa Fe's mainline to Pasadena. In the early 1970s my parents, Jill and Charles Lawrence, took me on weekend "vacations" to the Mojave Desert outpost of Barstow, driving Route 66 and following the Santa Fe–Union Pacific mainlines. We'd stay at the El Rancho Barstow motel and play in the pool during the hot afternoons; in the relative cool of the early evening, we'd drive to the big Santa Fe classification yard and locomotive shops and take pictures of the handsome blue and yellow diesels.

Some people spend their weekends in Lake Tahoe or Las Vegas. Others head to the mountains or the beaches. We drove to Barstow. This book was my destiny.

Until March of 2000, I was never far from either 66 or the Santa Fe, which eventually lost its identity in the 1995 merger with Burlington Northern. A series of moves finally led us to the California Bay Area . . . but in a poetic twist of fate we landed in Salinas, home of author John Steinbeck, who made Route 66 famous with his landmark novel, *The Grapes of Wrath*. God couldn't have sent a better sign that it was time to make *Route 66 Railway* a reality.

While countless authors and photographers have told the individual stories of these fabled routes, this is the first serious exploration of their relationship. It's true, Santa Fe was not the only railroad to follow Route 66—east of New Mexico, the highway encountered a patchwork of rail lines on its way to Chicago, including the Alton, the Frisco, and the Rock Island. But no other railroad has followed the highway for as many miles, or shared so many historic par-

allels and cultural touchstones. They also share the American Southwest, which marks the spiritual heart and soul of their relationship and adds considerably to the mythos.

In the early years of this project, a strong sense of urgency fueled every trip. The relics of the old highway seemed to be slipping away. Motels, cafes, and tourist stops appeared forgotten and crumbling. At the time, less than ten years had passed since the final stretch of U.S. 66 was bypassed in Williams, Arizona. A dedicated group of individuals were working to save what remained, but Route 66's future was uncertain at best.

In the later years of this project, a newfound sense of urgency emerged—now I found myself rushing to catch various structures before they received a new coat of paint, or a bright "Historic Route 66" sign. Nostalgia and international tourism brought the road back from the brink; Americans weary of fast food and corporate chains are slowly returning to rediscover the historic treasure we almost abandoned.

On the flip side, the Santa Fe Railway had reached its economic and visual peak during the early 1990s, with fleets of container trains led by state-of-the-art locomotives wearing red and silver "Warbonnet" colors. By the early 2000s, the merged BNSF Railway would result in a staggering number of trains alongside the Mother Road. Sadly, the last vestiges of the old Santa Fe continue to slip away, but today's BNSF is as good as contemporary railroading gets.

Still, the story is far from over. Many physical legacies of road and railroad face ongoing dangers. As this Introduction was being finalized, the historic "Harvey House" railroad station complex in Seligman, Arizona, faced imminent demolition. The El Vado Motel in Albuquerque was recently saved from a similar fate, but its future is by no means secure. The harsh truth is that many small towns

along the old road lack the financial resources to save their treasures—be they motel, train station, cafe, or any other quirky building that no longer fits the homogenized, harried lifestyle of today's America. Much of what has been accomplished is due largely to a relatively small band of people who long ago decided to save the Mother Road from slipping away. Thankfully, they have recognized and included the Santa Fe's proud heritage in their efforts.

This book is an effort to share 17 years of photographic passion. It's designed to equally delight fans of railroading, of roadside America, and of the great Southwest. Most of all, it celebrates a relationship that has brought us eight decades of memories, with many more yet to come.

John Steinbeck wrote in *Travels with Charley: In Search of America* that "people don't take trips—trips take people." I hope you enjoy the trip.

ELROND LAWRENCE
SALINAS, CALIFORNIA

Above: Jackrabbit, 1993
Right: Station detail, San Bernardino

Two Men Named Cyrus

"How will we know it's us without our past?"
— JOHN STEINBECK, *The Grapes of Wrath*

In 1926, two events marked the beginning of a beautiful friendship.

On November 11, a committee of federal and state highway officials commissioned U.S. Highway 66 from Chicago to Los Angeles. Spanning eight states, the newly christened highway united a patchwork of existing roads that included the National Old Trails route, assorted other trails, and countless unnamed dirt roads.

Three days later, on November 14, the Atchison, Topeka & Santa Fe Railway inaugurated the *Chief*, an extra fare, all-Pullman luxury train that quickly became the railroad's new flagship between the same two cities.

Both events were milestones in American transportation history. Few realized at the time how the Santa Fe and Route 66 would go on to become icons of travel, and how the developments of November 1926 would set in motion a relationship that would continue for eight decades. It would take time for either route to fashion its mystique.

Symbols of a historic relationship: Route 66 signs stand in downtown Chicago, Illinois, within sight of Santa Fe's former headquarters building at 80 East Jackson Boulevard.

Train No. 20, the *Chief*, noses across Colorado Boulevard in Pasadena, California, in August 1958. Santa Fe's Second District crossed this early alignment of Route 66 until the rail line was closed in 1994.

Santa Fe had been carrying passengers between Los Angeles and Chicago for nearly 40 years at the time of Route 66's christening. American traders first arrived in this land in 1821, when Captain William Becknell led them across what would become the Santa Fe Trail. Then, the town of Santa Fe was the seat of government and business center for the Spanish territory of New Mexico. Eventually Mexico would break free of Spain's control, but it would ultimately cede New Mexico to the United States in 1848.

Trade and travel quickly grew over the Santa Fe Trail, and that caught the eye of a Kansas businessman named Cyrus K. Holliday. In 1860, Holliday and others organized the Atchison & Topeka Railroad Company, with Holliday named the first president; three years later, the Atchison, Topeka & Santa Fe Railroad was born. In 1869, the railroad's first locomotive—a 4-4-0 type named after Holliday—pulled a two-car train over the first seven miles of completed track in Kansas. At a company picnic, the locomotive's namesake would predict that AT&SF would ultimately connect Chicago, St. Louis, and Galveston with San Francisco and Mexico City.

Following Holliday's pivotal speech, events began to move quickly: the Santa Fe, in concert with affiliate and subsidiary companies, began to spread its web of steel across the Midwest, reaching out to Kansas City, the Texas interior, Chicago, and finally crossing the Kansas-Colorado border westward to reach Pueblo, Colorado. On December 7, 1878, the first Santa Fe train rolled into New Mexico via Raton Pass, then the only practical rail route from Colorado. In a stroke of irony, the AT&SF mainline would never reach its namesake city of Santa Fe, as engineers deemed the terrain too difficult; instead, the capital city would be served by an 18-mile branchline that left the main route at Lamy, New Mexico.

In spring 1880, the railroad reached Albuquerque. Santa Fe had passed through the gates of the Southwest, and California was firmly in its sights. A flurry of short lines were being built in the Golden State, and all that remained for AT&SF was to build across western New Mexico and northern Arizona before reaching the California border at the Colorado River. To finish the job, Santa Fe acquired half of the Atlantic & Pacific Railroad Company—a franchise chartered by Congress to build from Albuquerque along

Above: No. 1254 leads a westbound passenger train through Arizona's Kingman Canyon circa 1910. National Old Trails Highway, seen at right, eventually became U.S. 66; in 1923 Santa Fe built a second track that followed the cliffs and crossed above the road.

Left: A lonely outpost in California's vast Mojave Desert, Ludlow served as headquarters for the Tonopah & Tidewater Railroad and its junction with the Santa Fe. Long before Route 66, an eastbound passenger train curved into town circa 1910.

Atlantic & Pacific Railroad Company
Office of General Manager

D. B. Robinson,
General Manager.

Albuquerque, N.M.   Dec. 26th, 1885.

A. & P. R. R.
NO ANSWER.
JAN 1 1886
PRESIDENT.

A. & P. R. R.
RECEIVED.
JAN 1 1886
PRESIDENT.

Col. H. C. Nutt,

President Atlantic & Pacific R. R.,

Boston,   Mass.

Dear Sir:-

Referring to your note of December 3rd.   I will

change the name of Waterman Junction to Barstow by circular Janu-

ary 1st, and have asked Mr. Victor of the California Southern to

do the same.

Yours truly,

General Manager.

Atlantic & Pacific Railroad Co.,

General Superintendent's Office,
ALBUQUERQUE, N. M.

Bridge

file together

MEMORANDUM.

25th. November, 1884.

H. C. Nutt Esq.

President, Boston.

RECEIVED
DEC 5 '84
H.C.NUTT.

RECEIVED
DEC 1 '84
H.C.NUTT.

Dear Sir:

Referring to your favor of the 19th. inst., I have just

received a telegram from the S.P. foreman at the Colorado River,

copy of
informing that the bridge is completed.   I enclose you a letter

from Chief Engineer Drake, of date the 24th. inst., relative to

the bridge.

Yours Truly

General Superintendent.

1 Enclosure.

Atlantic & Pacific memos announced
the completion of the Colorado River
crossing in 1884, and the renaming
of Waterman Junction to Barstow in
January 1886.

Santa Fe used a 1903 *Out West*
advertisement to promote its
California Limited service, with what
may be the first link between the
railway and the numbers "66."

An aerial view of Ash Fork, Arizona—once a key railroad junction for Santa Fe's routes to Los Angeles and Phoenix—illustrates how the road and railroad served as lonely lifelines for the dusty towns of the Southwest.

the 35th parallel to the Colorado River, and eventually the Pacific Ocean. Despite holding valuable land grants, the A&P was owned by the St. Louis & San Francisco Railway, which lacked the financial capital to build to California. That all changed when Santa Fe and its greater resources entered the picture. The two railroads split ownership, and the A&P was ready to fulfill its charter.

A morning ceremony on April 8, 1880, broke ground for the Atlantic & Pacific's new Western Division. Under the direction of chief engineer Henry Holbrook, and later Lewis Kingman, the railroad would build 560 miles across a generally inhospitable and largely uninhabited land. Three years would pass before the A&P would cross the Arizona Divide and close the gap between the Rio Grande and Colorado rivers.

Atlantic & Pacific crews reached the banks of the Colorado in 1883 to discover that the Southern Pacific Railroad was waiting for them—with a completed railroad from Mojave to The Needles, just across the river. The SP had made huge investments in its northern and southern transcontinental routes into California, and saw any encroachment as a serious threat. SP's new "Colorado Division" was designed solely to block the A&P's entry into the state.

Two months after the A&P arrived on the Colorado's east bank, a bridge was completed across the river and the railroads were joined with little fanfare. SP routinely turned away interchange traffic and delivered precious little freight to the A&P route. As the standoff ensued, the Western Division effectively became a grand railroad to nowhere. The stalemate was finally broken when Santa Fe marshaled forces to begin building an A&P line that would parallel the SP across the Mojave. Faced with the prospect of owning a worthless desert route, SP agreed to a deal and eventually sold its Colorado Division to the Santa Fe.

In November 1885, another key puzzle piece fell into place when Santa Fe subsidiary California Southern finished a rail line through Southern California's Cajon Pass, connecting with the A&P at Waterman Junction (later renamed Barstow in honor of Santa Fe president William Barstow Strong). Santa Fe trains could now travel from Kansas City to the Pacific Coast port of San Diego, via the

Above: Tourism was alive and well in the early years of the 20th century. Prehistoric cliff dwellings, lava beds, the San Francisco Peaks, and other attractions vied for visitors' attention in downtown Flagstaff, Arizona, circa 1915.

Right: Highway travelers rest on the California side of the Colorado River crossing during the late 1940s. The 1890 Red Rock Bridge was a former railroad bridge until Santa Fe built a new deck structure in 1945.

California Southern route. However, Santa Fe decided to lease Southern Pacific track into Los Angeles, and soon purchased the Los Angeles & San Gabriel Valley Railroad via Pasadena.

Santa Fe finally had the west coast market it had dreamed of, and the first transcontinental train arrived in Los Angeles on May 31, 1887. Further acquisitions would provide a crucial link from Kansas City, Kansas, to Chicago, and Americans would soon be able to travel exclusively on Santa Fe trains between the Windy City and the City of Angels.

However, in its earliest years, train travel across the Southwest was a miserable experience; passengers were at the mercy of railroad employees who cooperated with shady restaurant owners at station stops, taking their money in advance, and giving them food that ranged from barely edible to rancid (and in many cases, no food at all).

But this all changed with a partnership between Santa Fe officials and Fred Harvey, an English-born entrepreneur and a former employee of the Chicago, Burlington & Quincy Railroad. Harvey had been a victim of these conniving trainmen and trackside eateries. He saw an opportunity to change the system and introduce a new level of dining standards. In 1876, he operated a lunchroom in Topeka, Kansas, based on a handshake; two years later, he contracted with AT&SF to operate a restaurant and hotel at Florence, Kansas, again bearing the Harvey standard of fine food in a comfortable setting.

His continued success in Kansas triggered a chain of restaurants and hotels—"Harvey Houses"—that opened along the Santa Fe lines all the way to California. In some cases, the fledgling restaurants started out as little more than simple frame houses or strings of box cars. Once inside, however, guests were awed by furnishings, food, and service equal to any five-star resort.

Harvey's first lunch and dining room in the Southwest was in Raton, New Mexico, and the first hotel was the Montezuma in Las Vegas, New Mexico; both opened during 1882. (The Montezuma closed in 1903, replaced by the 1899-built Castañeda.) Eventually, the Fred Harvey Company would operate more than 20 hotels and every single lunch counter and dining room along the Santa Fe system. These were

the homes of the "Harvey Girls"—young women brought west by Harvey to serve as the waitress staff for each of his establishments. The phrase "Meals by Fred Harvey" revolutionized the Santa Fe travel experience and unknowingly paved the way for standardized meals and lodging that today's travelers take for granted.

An economic depression in 1893 drained Santa Fe's revenues, forcing the railroad into bankruptcy. The company emerged as the reorganized AT&SF Railway, and quickly built a reputation for speed and luxury, coupled with unmatched service by Fred Harvey and framed by the grandeur of the American Southwest. Recognizing Americans' fascination with that exotic land, the railway's marketing department stamped views of red cliffs and Native Americans onto timetables, postcards, and brochures—painting a Santa Fe trip as a grand, romantic adventure, experienced from the comfort (and safety) of a Pullman car. In that pioneering era of Southwest travel, Santa Fe's earliest luxury trains included the *DeLuxe* and the *California Limited* . . . the latter boasting a travel time in 1903 that featured a soon-to-be-familiar number: 66 hours between Los Angeles and Chicago.

Above: With the advent of on-board rail dining, the Fred Harvey Company shifted its focus to the motoring public. A Harvey House billboard entices weary Route 66 travelers near Seligman, Arizona, in the later years of the restaurant and hotel chain.

Opposite: Fred Harvey touring cars gather beside Santa Fe's passenger depot at Lamy, New Mexico, circa 1930.

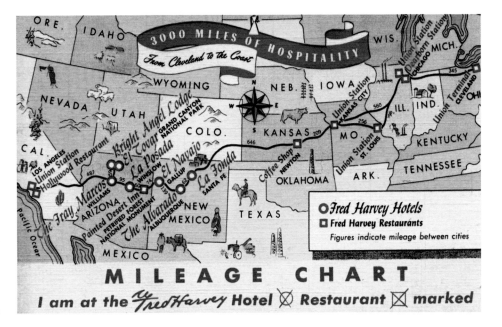

Left: Fred Harvey's chain of hotels and restaurants linked the Santa Fe with the towns it served.

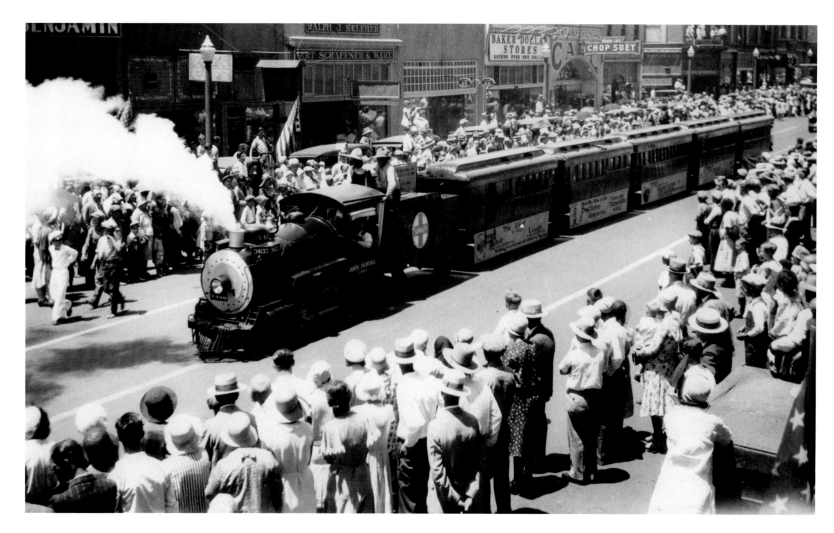

Cyrus K. Holliday passed away in 1900, but he had lived to see his dream come true: Santa Fe had reached the Pacific Coast, as well as Chicago and the Gulf Coast. Fred Harvey passed away the following year, his name synonymous with travel elegance and his hospitality empire ever expanding. As the Southwest grew and its towns evolved, Santa Fe trains became bigger, faster, and more civilized, led by the flagship *California Limited*. And yet America was changing again, the cycle of progress accelerating with the debut of the motor car.

Above: Other than streetcars, Route 66 drivers never had to share the road with rail traffic. A delightful exception took place when Santa Fe sponsored an entry in Albuquerque, New Mexico's Jubilee Parade, seen steaming down Central Avenue about 1930.

Right: Santa Fe No. 5028, one of the railway's magnificent 2-10-4 "Texas" type locomotives, steams past the locomotive shops in Albuquerque, New Mexico, in 1951.

"I challenge anyone to show a road of equal length that traverses more scenery, more agricultural
wealth, and more mineral wealth than does U.S. 66."

— CYRUS AVERY, "Father" of Route 66

Good roads had been sought since the 1800s, but railroads put that desire on hold with the completion of their westward expansion and the availability of fast, affordable travel. But the success of magnates like Henry Ford and the popularity of automobiles renewed the outcry for better roads. The federal government passed the Federal Aid Road Act of 1916, which made funds for new highways available to the states—encouraging cooperation between local and state officials in choosing routes and building roads. By 1920, three million miles of highways existed across the country, but most were fit only for horse and buggy. Only about 36,000 miles were surfaced properly to accommodate motor cars; the "network" of roads was an archaic mishmash of tracks, trails, and paths, established over the decades by Native Americans and pioneers.

Trains were the safest, most comfortable way to travel, but the automobile had sparked Americans' imagination. So Congress developed the Federal Highway Act of 1921, which called for a system of interconnected interstate highways. States would have to designate up to seven percent of their roads as national highways, if they wanted

High on the Arizona Divide, snowstorms transform the Coconino National Forest into a winter wonderland. An exceptional blizzard in December 1967 blanketed both road and railroad. In the aftermath, Santa Fe No. 1715 leads an eastbound freight out of Flagstaff while the Mother Road lies in virgin snow near Winona.

The popularity of Route 66 and train radios spelled the end for small-town train stations like those at Peach Springs, Arizona, and Thoreau, New Mexico, seen here during the mid-1960s.

Left: Santa Fe train No. 123 rolls beside the Mojave River in Victorville, California, in November 1964. Route 66 paralleled the tracks into the old downtown, and then turned southwest on its journey to Cajon Pass and the Los Angeles Basin.

to keep their federal financial ties. It was then that the country's strongest proponent of a Chicago-to-Los Angeles route emerged—Cyrus Stevens Avery, known today as the "Father of Route 66."

A Tulsa, Oklahoma, businessman, Avery had for years demonstrated a desire to see better highways in his state. With a federal highway system looming, he saw his chance to not only develop good roads for the region but also for the country. In 1921 he was elected president of the Associated Highways Association of America, and subsequently appointed state highway commissioner of Oklahoma in 1923. He also acted as the first chairman of the three-member State Highway Commission, which laid out the state highway system and dealt with maintenance and installing highway markers.

All of this was prelude, however, to Avery's pivotal appointment as leader of the American Association of State Highway Officials. As its annual 1924 meeting, the association—of which Avery emerged as leader—petitioned the Secretary of Agriculture to underwrite the selection and designation of a comprehensive system of interstate routes. Avery was charged to oversee the creation of the United States Highway System and map the most important routes. In 1925, he and others began to select existing state roads for the proposed network.

Thanks to his political savvy and experience with regional infighting, he was able to shrug off the traditional northern route via the Santa Fe Trail, and a southern route that followed the old Butterfield Stage Line. Avery's highway would head south from Chicago to Missouri, but instead of bearing west, it would escape the Rocky Mountains by angling farther south through a corner of Kansas and through his home state of Oklahoma. From Tulsa, the highway would point west through Texas, New Mexico, Arizona, and California.

Kingman Explosion

Route 66's proximity to a busy railroad has always carried an element of danger, but few accidents rival the horrific events of July 5, 1973, in Kingman, Arizona. As workers unloaded a tank car filled with propane at the east end of town, a hose coupling failed and the leaking gas ignited. Hank Graham, then a 30-year-old brakeman for Santa Fe, was riding an eastbound local that afternoon; as their train approached the Doxol Gas Western Energy plant, they spotted the tanker jetting a tall stream of fire. Kingman's volunteer fire department arrived on the scene and began working to cool the car, despite 105-degree weather. But the heat was too great, and it erupted into a two-acre fireball. Twelve people were killed in the cataclysm, most of them firefighters, and over 100 others were injured. Graham had his camera and captured the terrible moment; he also photographed the aftermath as his train backed away from the scene. Several businesses along 66 were destroyed or damaged by flaming debris. The explosion continues to be Arizona's worst firefighting disaster and a sad milestone in Kingman's railroad history.

The nation's highway commissioners decided to assign numbers instead of names to the planned roads, and use even numbers for highways running east and west. Routes that crossed state lines would be given shield-shaped signs identifying them as U.S. highways. Main highways would be numbered under 100, and the more important roads would be designated as "zero numbers."

Avery and Midwest officials decided on Route 60 for the Chicago–Los Angeles route, but they faced harsh objections from Kentucky and Virginia, who supported their own highway linking Newport News, Virginia, with Springfield, Missouri, and wanted the number 60. Both sides refused to give in, and when Kentucky threatened to pull out of the highway network, Avery compromised, fearing Congress might scuttle the entire system. When he saw that the number 66 was available, he and other officials agreed it had a catchy sound. On November 11, 1926, after two years of planning, squabbling, and concessions, U.S. Highway 66 was official. Americans would eventually refer to the highway as simply "Route 66," which continues to this day.

The newly born highway would take time to assume its role as a transportation icon. Upon its commissioning, only 800 miles of the designated route were paved; another 11 years would pass before paving would be completed over its entire length. Moreover, many portions of the route took meandering (and in some cases, primitive) paths, limited by construction methods and equipment of the period. Ultimately, the highway would reach its final configuration of 2,448 miles through shedding hundreds of miles of roundabout, twisty, and sometimes treacherous portions.

Route 66 was unique in that it navigated a largely diagonal route, rather than the typical east-west directions of the era. More important, it fed into scores of tiny Midwest communities and gave them access to two of the nation's biggest cities, Chicago and Los Angeles. In the years ahead, this routing would become a lifeline to thousands of post-Depression Americans seeking a new future, and change the highway's role in ways its creators never imagined.

Along this fledgling route, through virtually every town, a railroad could be found. Railroads had built the

towns that anchored Route 66; their presence ensured each town's economic future. In the days before urban sprawl, when downtown served as the cultural center for a population, the train station was its centerpiece, a gateway to distant lands and the promise of a new life.

The highway would change this. No longer would Americans solely depend on steel rails and rigid schedules; motor cars allowed people to travel where they liked and when they liked, and the freedom to stop at any place they wished. Workers could live outside their cities and commute, farmers and other remote industries would no longer be isolated . . . the open road, like the railroad before it, held the promise of new life.

Reminders of the glory years:
An aging mileage marker stands near
Siberia, California; neon in Barstow,
California; a retired Santa Fe box car
at Hinkley, California.

Above: Seen from the foundations of the future Interstate 40, four elegant Alco PA diesels lead Train No. 8 across the Colorado River at Topock, Arizona, in November 1965.

Left: Warbonnets, the San Gabriel Mountains, and Arcadia's picturesque depot combine for an idyllic Southern California image in December 1964.

Opposite: What better way to see Route 66? Photographer Gordon Glattenberg creates a memorable view of Cajon Boulevard traffic at Ono, east of San Bernardino, California, in June 1957. The scene was captured from the cab of Santa Fe F3A No. 21, leading the return trip of a Los Angeles-Cajon Summit excursion.

Left: Leading a special Amtrak train, No. 5998 crossed the Pasadena Freeway at Highland Park, California, in 1987. Two years later, the rebuilt FP45 received red and silver colors as part of Santa Fe's "Super Fleet" marketing campaign.

Top right: Now boarded up, the Mohawk Mini-Mart in Oro Grande, California, was still selling gas in 1990 as Santa Fe 5301 East blasted by.

Even with the newfound freedom of the automobile, traveling across the arid Southwest by car was a formidable task, especially in the desert where some "roads" were little more than trails or a series of wooden planks. Trains were no longer the *only* means of travel, but they were clearly the best way to travel.

The 1926 launch of Santa Fe's first-class *Chief* would ensure this fact for decades to come. Clocking in at 63 hours between Los Angeles and Chicago, the *Chief* offered all-Pullman sleeping car service, as well as a maid, barber, valet, and other on-board services. The luxury train established Santa Fe's reputation for speed and service, enhanced by fine onboard dining from the Fred Harvey Company, and travel packages that bundled Harvey's trackside hotels and touring car excursions to popular Arizona destinations like the Grand Canyon, the Petrified Forest, and the Painted Desert.

The following year, Santa Fe took delivery of its first "Northern" locomotives—the 3751-class, built by Baldwin Locomotive Works. With big 4-8-4 wheel arrangements, the huge engines were assigned to the *Chief* and other popular trains, and the series launched Santa Fe's modern era of steam. The "class of 3751" is also notable for its

legacy: the first 4-8-4, No. 3751, was restored to service in 1991 by the San Bernardino Railroad Historical Society and still powers special trains (sister No. 3759 remains on display in Kingman's Locomotive Park).

Meanwhile, Cyrus Avery had turned to grassroots marketing to spread the word about the new highway. Shortly after announcing the creation of Route 66, Avery and Missourian John Woodruff organized the National U.S. 66 Highway Association, with officers from each of the eight states along the route. At the kickoff meeting, Avery suggested adopting the name "Main Street of America" to use on promotional brochures and maps. Route 66's first advertising campaign was under way. Great things seemed just around the corner for both the highway and railroad that ran between Los Angeles and Chicago.

However, less than three years after the milestones of 1926, the decade known as the Roaring Twenties lost its fire. America's economy began to falter, and eventually it collapsed along with the stock market. The Great Depression of 1929 would irrevocably change the railway and the highway; both would bear the scars of the nation's suffering, and each would emerge from the decade of the 1930s transformed physically and culturally.

Santa Fe's transformation came with the arrival of the diesel locomotive, even as steam-powered technology had reached its zenith on the AT&SF with the 1930 delivery of the powerful "Texas"-type 2-10-4 engines, numbered in the 5000 series. The first diesel, a switcher numbered 2300 from the Alco Locomotive Company of Schenectady, New York, rolled onto the property five years later. It was followed by two road diesels, a pair of box cabs numbered 1A and 1B, which would pull the first incarnation of the railroad's newest luxury train—the *Super Chief*, America's first diesel-powered, all Pullman sleeping car train.

The weekly *Super Chief* debuted in May 1936 with heavyweight cars, and boasted an amazing travel time of 39 hours and 45 minutes between Chicago and Los Angeles—a full business day better than the *Chief*'s 50-hour travel time. One year later, Santa Fe gave the train a total makeover, and re-launched it with stainless steel cars and streamlined E1 diesels that bore a striking new image: designed by Leland Knickerbocker of the Electro-Motive Corporation, the design featured a silver body capped by a red and yellow nose, with the red curving around the cab like the feathers of an Indian chief's headdress. An instant classic, the "Warbonnet" had arrived. The livery perfectly symbolized the railroad's embracing of the Southwest and the Native American people, and it would become one of the world's most famous railroad images. The Warbonnet would forever be associated with the Santa Fe name, and it would leave a lasting memory on every child who ever owned a Lionel train set.

The *Super Chief* quickly became Santa Fe's new standard-bearer, and the railroad would quickly double its weekly frequency with the purchase of a second train consist. Other name trains like the *El Capitan* would follow, and the popularity of both it and the *Super Chief* eventually warranted daily service. Inspired by these trains, the railway ramped up its stylish Southwest marketing campaign, further embracing the region's Native American heritage. Timetable covers and magazine ads debuted the image of a young Indian boy gazing at a red and silver train while writing in the sand, "Santa Fe All the Way." In New Mexico,

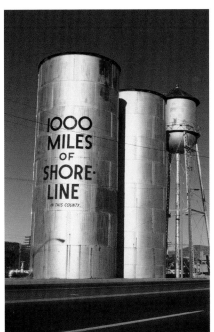

Left: Today they announce Kingman's Route 66 heritage, but during the 1980s the former Santa Fe water tanks wore a decidedly different slogan.

Above: Bagdad, California, was once a locomotive helper base and a Route 66 town, but had withered away by the 1970s.

506—Santa Fe's "Super Chief" Traveling thru the Orange Groves, California

© CURT TEICH & CO., INC.   OB-H678

KITE SHAPED TRACK

Santa Fe

Far left: Vintage *Super Chief* post-cards helped cultivate the California mystique.

Left: The "Kite Shaped Track" referred to Santa Fe's rail network throughout Southern California in the early 20th century. A traveler could ride from Los Angeles to San Bernardino and Redlands, then return via a southern route through Riverside and Fullerton.

"Indian Detours" ferried Santa Fe passengers by "Harvey Car" to the state's many pueblos and reservations, basing the tours out of Fred Harvey resorts like the El Navajo Hotel in Gallup or the La Fonda Hotel in Santa Fe. No other railroad was so influenced by the territory it served, or embraced the culture of its land so closely.

But while the *Super Chief* helped Santa Fe capture the excitement (and dollars) of the traveling public, the Depression continued to rage on. Hit particularly hard were farmers in the Midwest and the Southeast, assaulted by unprecedented droughts that began in 1930 and lasted several years. The infamous Dust Bowl triggered giant black dust storms that swept away the crops and the livelihoods of farmers who had lived off the land for generations. Once the fields were blown away, corporate bankers and their agents descended to collect whatever remained.

Thus began the flight of the poor and disenfranchised to the "promised land" of California, and Route 66 was their escape route. Okies, Kansans, and Texans piled every-thing they owned into rickety motor vehicles and poured onto the highway, fueled by dreams of fertile fields and a new life. This migration spawned author John Steinbeck's Pulitzer Prize-winning 1939 novel, *The Grapes of Wrath*, centered on the Joad family and its harrowing journey across the Southwest. In it, he gave Route 66 a new, iconic name—the "Mother Road."

While Santa Fe revamped its image with Warbonnet diesels and streamlined trains, Route 66 underwent some streamlining of its own. The paving of the entire highway had taken over a decade to accomplish, and during the process, some sections were bypassed by newly built roads. One significant change involved a route through the railway's namesake city of Santa Fe, plus Raton and Glorieta passes, which was replaced in 1937 by a direct stretch into Albuquerque by way of Santa Rosa. West of the city, a southern route that followed the Santa Fe mainline via Los Lunas to Correo was also shed.

In California, a winding portion of the highway through the railroad town of Goffs, California, was replaced by a direct stretch of pavement between Essex and Needles in 1931. The Los Angeles region experienced a series of changes and re-routes: early Route 66 in Pasadena once crossed the Santa Fe as part of Colorado Boulevard, then continued to Los Angeles via the curving Colorado Street Bridge and Figueroa; the final version would turn south just east of the crossing and follow the Santa Fe into Los Angeles as the Arroyo Seco Parkway (California's first freeway). Aside from these major changes, scores of re-routings were made to trim the highway's mileage, rid it of flood-prone sections, and eliminate dangerous curves and other obstacles.

The end of the Dust Bowl and the start of World War II brought a surge of military traffic to both the railroad and the highway, and stretched the limits of each with convoys and troop trains. Bus and train stations filled with servicemen shuttling between bases, and roadside businesses prospered once again, even as they weathered gas rationing and other wartime conditions. The sudden rise in railroad passengers was a boon to the Harvey House restaurants and hotels, which were hit hard by the Depression. Many of the grand buildings faced closures and cutbacks during the 1930s, as passengers gravitated to onboard dining car service, but the war gave them a new lease on life.

Following World War II, Route 66 was again alive with convoys of vehicles—this time, shiny autos filled with postwar G.I.s and their families on the move. The country had regained its optimism, and that spirit fueled a westward movement by Americans eager to start a new life. So heavy was highway traffic that the migration actually surpassed the Dust Bowl exodus. One of those cars contained songwriter Bobby Troup, who was driving from Pennsylvania to Los Angeles to relaunch his musical career after a stint in the war. Early in the trip, his wife had suggested the idea of a song about a highway, and somewhere west of St. Louis she whispered in his ear, "Get your kicks on Route 66."

"God, what a marvelous idea of a song!" Troup would later recall. He took out a ruler to measure the distance from Chicago to L.A., and closely studied the many towns

and landmarks along the way to California. Not long after arriving in Los Angeles, he completed his "musical map" of the highway. Troup eventually played the bluesy tune for his idol, the great Nat "King" Cole, who loved the song and turned it into a 1946 single. "Get Your Kicks on Route 66" would become one of Cole's biggest pop hits; since the song's release, it's been covered by literally hundreds of bands, including the Rolling Stones, Chuck Berry, and Depeche Mode, and it most recently appeared in the animated movie *Cars*.

Ironically, Santa Fe was given its own catchy tune earlier that same year, courtesy of Hollywood songwriters Johnny Mercer and Harry Warren. In January 1946, MGM Studios released its musical *The Harvey Girls*, starring Judy Garland and Ray Bolger. Set in an idealized vision of the Southwest, the movie told the story of Fred Harvey's famous waitress staff and their adventures beside the railroad. The highlight of the film, however, was its show-stopping production number, "On the Atchison, Topeka and the Santa Fe," which went on to win an Oscar for best song.

Sadly, as moviegoers flocked to see a Harvey House in theaters, few were traveling to the actual establishments. The wartime rush was over, and twilight had fallen upon the hotels and eating houses that physically linked the railroad and Route 66. The hotels closed en masse, followed by many of the restaurants. Several eating houses survived as lunchrooms, but most were abandoned to the care of AT&SF for office use, or they were donated to local cities.

The 1950s marked the last flourish for Route 66 and the Santa Fe Railway. Both had matured in technology and style, and neither would again look this good. Santa Fe's steam locomotives were retired by 1957, leaving colorful diesels in charge—the public "face" of the fleet was best illustrated by hundreds of rounded-nose F-unit models from General Motors' Electro-Motive Division, plus sleek PA-1s from the Alco Locomotive Company. A myriad of freight diesels, including road-switchers and yard engines, completed the motive power menu. Lightweight, stainless steel cars dominated the passenger fleet, including luxurious new dome-lounges, diners, and curved-end observation cars.

In 1956, Santa Fe unveiled its boldest concept yet—the Hi-level passenger car, a double-decker design that gave travelers a towering view of the Southwest. Touted by "Chico" (the railroad's Indian boy mascot) in magazine ads, the Hi-levels were the forerunner of Amtrak's modern "Superliner" cars. A handful of ex-Santa Fe cars still roll along the Pacific Coast on Amtrak's popular *Coast Starlight* between Los Angeles and Seattle.

Meanwhile, the towns built by the A&P found themselves along the "Main Street of America," propelled to unimagined prosperity by thousands of Americans on the road. Depots and downtown districts competed with neon-lit motor courts, cafes, and service stations that sprung up along the main drags, beckoning travelers with neon artistry and wacky gimmicks—wigwam motels, gigantic arrows, mountain lion zoos, fiberglass jackrabbits, blue swallows, and enough dinosaurs to fill the movie *Jurassic Park*. Scenic attractions like the Grand Canyon and Petrified Forest added to the allure of a Route 66 vacation, as did California destinations like Disneyland, but it was the outlandish marketing stunts that sealed the deal for many a sedan filled with squealing kids. The great American adventure west was now a parade of happy families that raced red and silver *Chiefs* around mesas, through canyons and forests, and across the deserts.

> **"Life doesn't happen along the interstates.**
> **It's against the law."**
>
> — WILLIAM LEAST HEAT-MOON, travel writer

However, as the fifties rolled on, forces were at work for a new travel system that would push both the railroad and the highway to the brink of oblivion. President Dwight Eisenhower had witnessed the German autobahn during his time in World War II; smitten, he enacted the Federal Aid Highway Act of 1956, which mapped out a 42,500-mile national interstate system. Despite the expansion of many stretches into modern four-lane highways, 66 simply could no longer handle the increasing traffic.

As interstate construction began, the National U.S. 66 Highway Association tried to prevent the road's total

destruction, even asking at one point for the new freeway to be called I-66 (that "honor" was given to a stretch from Virginia to Washington, D.C.). Twelve years were planned to complete the interstate, but it took more than twice as long. Route 66 was replaced by five interstate routes: I-55 from Chicago, Illinois, to St. Louis, Missouri; I-44 from St. Louis to Oklahoma City, Oklahoma; I-40 from Oklahoma City to Barstow, California; I-15 from Barstow to San Bernardino, California; and I-10 from San Bernardino to Santa Monica, California.

The effects were devastating. Rail travel, which had already been in decline thanks to the American car craze, fell into a downward spiral as the interstate progressed. Though Santa Fe refused to lower its service standards like some other railroads, the railway dropped many of its passenger trains in 1967, leaving only a handful of name trains:

Above: Kingman's ties to road and railroad are apparent as Santa Fe 4000 East emerges from Kingman Canyon, Arizona, in 1993.

Right: Santa Rosa, New Mexico

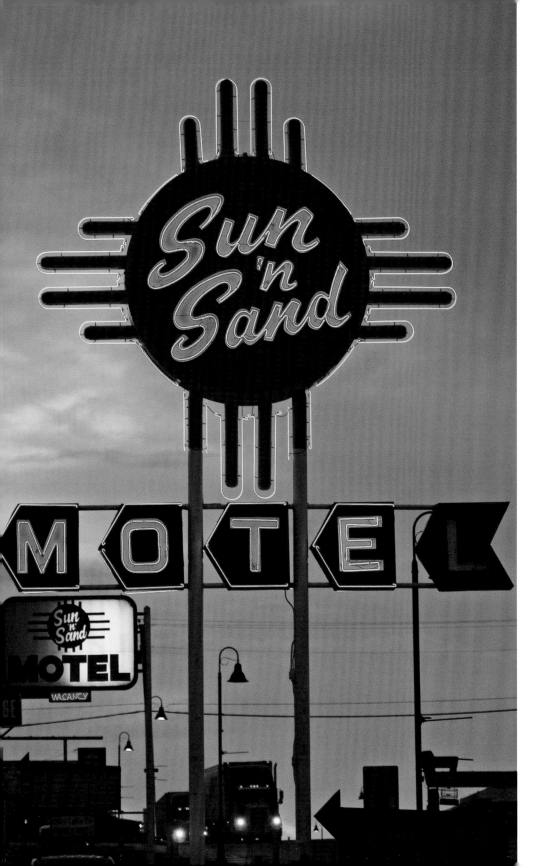

the *Texas Chief*, the *San Francisco Chief*, the *El Capitan*, the popular *San Diegans*, and, of course, the flagship *Super Chief*. However, the *Super Chief* and the *El Capitan* would be combined into a single train except during peak seasons. The landmark *Chief* fell into history, its last run being May 13, 1968; that December, Fred Harvey operation of dining cars came to a close.

Santa Fe placed a few last orders for dedicated passenger locomotives in the 1960s—most notably nine FP45 diesels dressed in Warbonnet red and silver—but the writing was on the wall. The U.S. Postal Service pulled its railway express cars from Santa Fe passenger trains, leaving precious little revenue to justify continued service. Finally, in 1971, the United States government created Amtrak and relieved the railroads of their money-losing trains. The Warbonnet was retired, in favor of a similar livery in Santa Fe's blue and yellow freight colors. The remaining Harvey Houses closed across the system, with a handful surviving as lunch houses for freight crews.

For the first time in its history, Santa Fe was a freight-only railroad.

The interstate's impact on Route 66 would be equally harsh, but the road's demise would take far longer to complete. In the early 1960s, the highway was still an American icon that captured the country's imagination . . . it even spawned its own television show, *Route 66*, in 1960. The drama followed Buz and Tod, heroes who spurned the luxury of extra consonants, and their adventures across the country in a shiny Corvette. The show lasted four seasons; contrary to popular belief, the classic 'Vettes used for filming weren't red, but rather a series of blue and brown models, which photographed better in black and white.

Unfortunately, fame wasn't enough to save the real Route 66. During the 1970s and early 1980s, the Mother Road was replaced section-by-section, bypassing old stretches of asphalt and transforming them into front-age roads that served their successor. Shield signs were auctioned off. Roadmaps were changed. In 1977, 51 years after the road's commissioning, "End of Route 66" signs were removed from the eastern terminus in Chicago. Finally, on October 13, 1984, the last surviving segment of the highway in Williams, Arizona, was bypassed by Interstate 40. The next year, U.S. Highway 66 was officially decommissioned.

At the time, travelers celebrated. Few mourned the passing of the great trains or the end of the old highway. Interstate cheerleaders boasted how Americans could theoretically drive from one coast to another without ever stopping. This was progress, they said . . . but progress came at a price. Dozens of towns were circumvented and forgotten. Many saw their fortunes change in a single day: dozens of taillights followed the sunset through town one night, but the next day dawned upon an empty Main Street. America began its cultural progression to reduced human contact, standardization in favor of individuality, and the trading of personality for convenience.

Still, for many of the Southwest towns built by the Atlantic & Pacific, another cruel blow remained. In their battle with trucking lines, railroads turned increasingly to automation during the seventies and eighties, and Santa Fe was a leader in modernization. Old towns that grew up with the railroad lost their economic bases with the closing of division offices, crew-change points, and major locomotive and car repair shops in cities like San Bernardino and Albuquerque. Trains themselves lost a little of their romance with the end of cabooses, replaced by small flashing rear-end devices.

In 1985, the Santa Fe name itself was threatened, when the railway proposed a merger with rival Southern Pacific, going so far as to set aside its blue and yellow colors and paint hundreds of locomotives in a red, yellow, and black design. But the Interstate Commerce Commission scuttled the merger plans, and Santa Fe regrouped to face the 1990s. To do so, it would turn back to its storied history and revive a famous image.

In 1989, Santa Fe painted three of its veteran FP45 passenger diesels—now used for freight service and occasional directors' trains—in an updated version of the red and silver Warbonnet; the only significant change were big billboard "Santa Fe" letters that replaced the black script on the flanks. The revived colors were the brainchild of then-president Michael Haverty, who recognized their his-

toric and aesthetic appeal, and made them the centerpiece of a new "Super Fleet" marketing campaign. From 1990 to 1995, all new Santa Fe locomotives would be painted in gleaming red and silver, thrilling railfans, employees, and the general public.

The 1990s ushered in an era of corporate "mega-mergers," and railroads were swept up in the climate. Santa Fe again began merger talks with a major western railroad—the Burlington Northern, itself a combination of western roads that included the Great Northern, Northern Pacific, Chicago, Burlington & Quincy, the Spokane, Portland & Seattle, and the Santa Fe's former ally, the St. Louis-San Francisco Railway. This time the merger was approved, and in 1995 the Burlington Northern Santa Fe Railway was born, favoring the initials BNSF.

As the AT&SF name faded, another historic name was rising from the ashes. Angel Delgadillo, a barber in tiny Seligman, Arizona, had watched his town begin to die when the interstate bypassed it in 1978, and again when the Santa Fe closed its division offices in 1985. Recognizing the power of nostalgia and myth, Angel became one of the moving forces in the founding of the Historic Route 66 Association of Arizona. In 1987 the association successfully lobbied the state to designate and preserve Route 66 in Arizona as a historic highway. Following Arizona's lead, the other states along the highway also formed associations—California, New Mexico, Texas, Oklahoma, Kansas, Missouri, and Illinois.

By the late 1990s, the Route 66 mystique had captured the attention of international tourists, who quickly tired of the sameness of American interstates and their chain establishments. The influx of overseas travelers, combined with a rising nostalgia for small-town Americana, brought Route 66 back from the dead. Artists and authors flocked to the Mother Road, celebrating it with books, photography, and even movies; the 2006 Pixar movie *Cars* was set in the fictional town of Radiator Springs, but the town was squarely located beside the real Route 66. With public awareness at its highest in decades, many forgotten towns have reclaimed some or all of their tourist business, and

Santa Fe No. 100 is basking in her newly revived Warbonnet colors, just hours after the GP60M's maiden run from Chicago to Los Angeles in May 1990. The wildly popular colors were ultimately succeeded by the Great Northern-inspired "Heritage 1" scheme, modeled by BNSF No. 8601 in Needles, California.

the highway once again hosts carloads of travelers crossing the Southwest, bound for California like the migrants and vacationers of old.

The former Santa Fe mainline has also rebounded from the gloomy outlook of the seventies and early eighties. Today's BNSF boasts traffic levels unseen since World War II, thanks to highway congestion in big cities and a staggering volume of Pacific Rim imports that cross the United States by train. Up to 100 trains a day follow the Mother Road through California, Arizona, and New Mexico. Unfortunately, few of those trains still carry the iconic Warbonnet colors, as BNSF turned its back on what is arguably the country's most recognizable railroad image. Instead, the railway has tried three variations of an orange, green, and black design during the past decade, and while the look is hardly unattractive, it pales in comparison to the red and silver colors that generations of Americans fondly recall.

Amtrak also keeps the *Chief* name alive with its daily *Southwest Chief* trains that roll between Chicago and Los Angeles. While the passenger carrier seems to undergo an annual funding battle to survive, ridership continues to climb on trains 3 and 4, and the silver and blue trains are a welcome sight along the former Main Street of America.

The story isn't over, however: more work is needed to preserve the legacies of Route 66 and the former Santa Fe. The nonprofit World Monuments Fund recently added the highway to its list of the 100 most endangered cultural heritage sites worldwide. And while several Harvey Houses and depots along the route have been beautifully restored, many remain vulnerable to time and the elements. Even some restored structures sit largely vacant, as cities struggle to find the right tenants. Development is as much a danger as neglect; for example, the planned destruction of Albuquerque's El Vado Motel was recently halted by the city, but its fate is far from secure. Still, the road and its people have life and vitality again, all framed by the steady rumble of passing trains.

Looking back at more than 80 years of shared history, the parallels between the Santa Fe Railway and Route 66 are striking on many levels. Their physical proximity has always been obvious, but no one realized at the time how closely their histories intertwined. While it's easy to see today thanks to the luxury of passed time, it's no less remarkable how many cultural touchstones these two routes have shared. Each has experienced life, death, and rebirth. Once again, hope is on the horizon.

Given the perspective of eight decades, it's time to experience anew the legacy of two men named Cyrus. Unlike the Dust Bowl migrants and vacationers, we'll travel east, leaving the sprawl of Southern California behind as we venture up Cajon Pass, sprint across the desert, scale the Arizona divide, and thread the red cliffs of New Mexico. Pack up the car, bring plenty of water and snacks, and don't forget the cameras. The great Southwest awaits!

Ultra-modern BNSF No. 7606 departs Topock, Arizona, as the "beautiful friendship" continues into the 21st century.

California

For the traveler, California's eastern gateway is as far as one can get from idyllic postcard views of the state's orange groves, sunny beaches, and palm trees. After hours of descending the Arizona desert, a westbound *Super Chief* would round a curve at the old station of Topock and thunder onto a massive black bridge across the Colorado River, where passengers were simply greeted by the sweeping panorama of more desert.

With an even split of locomotive colors, a Santa Fe eastbound glides across the Colorado River as thunderclouds build across the Mojave.

Of course, first impressions are frequently deceiving. The crossing of the Colorado represented only a slice of California's scenic diversity. In a matter of hours the same rail passengers found themselves traversing the mountains through Cajon Pass, then pausing at the railroad town of San Bernardino before completing the final lap to Los Angeles. After so much time in the desert, the San Gabriel Valley must have seemed like paradise, with lush vineyards and groves of oranges, lemons, and grapefruit. Small towns dotted the final miles before Pasadena and elegant Los Angeles Union Station—towns such as Azusa and Cucamonga, which gained fame thanks to the Jack Benny show and "trainmaster" Mel Blanc's loud announcement: "Train leaving on Track Five for Anaheim, Azusa, and Cuuu-camonga!"

Like Santa Fe's streamliners, Route 66 quickly seared itself into the California consciousness. On its journey east to Chicago, 66 first encountered the Santa Fe in Pasadena, and the two lines paralleled each other to San Dimas. They drifted apart until San Bernardino, but east of town they became inseparable as they climbed out of the Los Angeles Basin and struck out across the desert.

Since then, development and urban sprawl have changed Southern California irrevocably. Groves and vineyards no longer follow the highway and the railroad east of San Dimas; instead, the towns of Rancho Cucamonga, Fontana, and Rialto have swelled into an endless sea of homes and shopping centers. Still, Route 66 remains largely intact across California except for an 18-mile section buried under Interstate 15 between Cajon Pass and Victorville. Meanwhile, Santa Fe's successor BNSF has evolved into a "super railroad," with a state-of-the-art physical plant and a staggering number of trains, dominated by container traffic to and from the ports of Long Beach and Los Angeles.

Bobby Troup may have rightly singled out Barstow and San Bernardino as places to "get your kicks," but there's also much to be said for the likes of Ludlow, Amboy, and Needles—towns that proudly display their railroad and Mother Road heritage in a forgotten corner of the Golden State.

PASADENA

Far from the desert is a Colorado crossing of a different kind—Santa Fe's intersection with Colorado Boulevard in Pasadena, best known for the Tournament of Roses Parade. From 1926 to 1931, westbound 66 drivers crossed the railroad before turning left on Fair Oaks Avenue. During the 1930s, the route continued west to the Colorado Street Bridge and Figueroa Street, preserving the physical Santa Fe–66 connection. In 1940, it was realigned via Arroyo Seco Parkway and the Pasadena Freeway into Los Angeles.

Just west of Arroyo Seco Parkway is the Pasadena depot, a Spanish Colonial Revival design erected in 1935. This was once home to Santa Fe's most glamorous station stop, as the *Super Chief* was the favorite train of Holly-

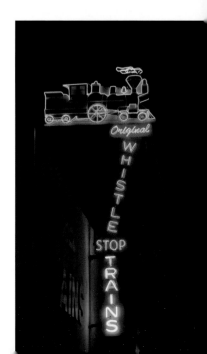

Above: Colorado Boulevard, 1992
Top left: *Super Chief* recreation
Left: Neon Whistle Stop sign

wood celebrities both in front of and behind the camera. Many stars boarded and detrained at Pasadena to elude the crowds at Los Angeles Union Passenger Terminal.

Completed in 1887, the Pasadena line between Los Angeles and San Bernardino was built in two phases by AT&SF affiliates: the Los Angeles & San Gabriel Valley and the San Bernardino & Los Angeles. Rail service lasted until 1994, when the rails were severed near Santa Anita. Between Los Angeles and Pasadena it's now the light-rail commuter "Gold Line," which burrows under Colorado Boulevard—making photos like GP60M No. 161 in downtown Pasadena into an unrepeatable scene. The most visible sign of railroading on Colorado Boulevard today is the neon sign for the "Original Whistle Stop" train store, a local fixture.

In February 1989, a surprise event relived the glory days of Pasadena railroading. Santa Fe used its old station in a filming sequence for its new "Super Fleet" marketing campaign, designed to recall the service standards of the *Super Chief*. Two ex–Santa Fe F7 diesels—Nos. 347 A & B, owned by the California State Railroad Museum in Sacramento—posed by the depot with a stainless steel train of Santa Fe business cars. A modern freight rolled by repeatedly for the cameras, but the crowd of onlookers knew who the *real* star was.

Little did fans know at the time that the "Super Fleet" would result in the return of the railroad's famous red and silver Warbonnet. All that mattered on this beautiful winter's day was an opportunity to see a California classic come to life, one last time.

FOOTHILL BOULEVARD

Route 66 is intact between Pasadena and San Bernardino, although urban traffic makes for a slow drive. The old Santa Fe line crosses the highway twice in Arcadia and Azusa, and the two routes close in together at Glendora, where the crew of a BNSF local stops at the Legends Diner for lunch. East of San Dimas, the highway becomes Foothill Boulevard and once played hide-and-seek with the Southern Pacific's Baldwin Park Branch, a former Pacific Electric interurban line. In 1987, two vintage "Espee" GP9Es cross Route 66 near Fontana. The line has since been abandoned but the bridge remains, not far from Bono's Italian restaurant and its historic "Mammoth Orange" stand.

At the eastern edge of San Bernardino lies the first of two surviving wigwam-style motor courts along Route 66, one of three nationwide. San Bernardino's Wigwam Motel was recently restored to its 1950s splendor—it's a far cry from previous decades when the motel's marquee read, "Do it in a Teepee."

Above: Wigwam Motel, San Bernardino
Bottom left: Mammoth Orange, Fontana
Below: Legends Diner, Glendora
Right: SP local, Foothill Boulevard

SAN BERNARDINO

Throughout the 20th century, San Bernardino was a vital point for Santa Fe's California Division. The town was home to locomotive shops, dispatching and administrative offices, switching yards, and a magnificent Mission Revival–style passenger station. The grand building was designed to reflect the city's image as the "gateway" to southern California. In the first half of the century, San Bernardino flourished in its role as a railroad town. At its heyday, nearly 85 percent of San Bernardino's residents depended on the railway for their livelihood.

As trains completed their descent of Cajon Pass and rolled into town, they could travel to Los Angeles via one of two routes: the Second District via Cucamonga and Pasadena, or the circuitous Third District via Riverside and Fullerton. Meanwhile, the sick and elderly of dieseldom rolled into the cavernous shops, and emerged with a new life and a fresh coat of paint.

Viaduct Park used to be the home of a Santa Fe steam survivor: No. 3751, the first 4-8-4 locomotive purchased by the railroad. The 1927 Baldwin was "evicted" in 1986 for a happy reason: the final stage of a ten-year restoration that returned the engine to action in 1991. Now based in Los Angeles, the historic engine is still owned by the San Bernardino Railroad Historical Society.

Left: San Bernardino depot
Top right: No. 3751 on display
Right: Santa Fe locomotive shops
Far right: Barber shop

As automobiles, trucks and air travel slowly eroded the railroad industry's dominance, San Bernardino's pillars began to crumble. The depot faded in importance after the arrival of Amtrak, reduced to serving only four daily trains; when Santa Fe's dispatching center and offices moved, the station fell into disrepair. In 1993, the historic shops closed and the work transferred to Topeka, Kansas, another victim of company consolidation. No longer needed, the shop buildings were demolished in 1995, replaced by a modern intermodal yard.

Route 66 touched the northwest corner of the shops before turning north on Mt. Vernon Avenue, where the landmark Santa Fe smokestack remains visible for miles. The station has been refurbished, and over 11,000 commuters each weekday board trains at the adjacent Metrolink commuter facility. The city has firmly grasped its Route 66 heritage, too—the annual "Route 66 Rendezvous" car cruise is wildly popular, attracting a quarter million people each year.

Cajon Boulevard is our route out of the San Bernardino Valley, and the former Route 66 provides several miles of side-by-side running with the former Santa Fe mainlines. Near Devore, we pass an ancient paved section of Route 66 that *predates* the highway's commissioning in 1926.

Left: Shops demolition
Right: Route 66 Rendezvous
Far right: AT&SF smokestack, 66 sign
Below: Early 66 alignment, Devore

CAJON PASS

The Union Pacific Railroad has trackage rights over Santa Fe's California gateway, adding to the variety of locomotive models and colors that parallel Route 66. Rolling beside Cajon Boulevard in 1984 is DDA40X No. 6943, a 98-foot leviathan of a locomotive that cranked out 6,600 horsepower. Turning our attention back to the road, the El Cajon Motel sign is a reminder of the highway's heritage.

Before we know it, we're climbing Cajon Pass, one of California's grandest railroad stages.

Trains have conquered Cajon for over 120 years, through heat waves, rainstorms, mudslides, fires, and the occasional snowfall. The latter is an occasion for weather-pampered Californians to unexpectedly call in sick and dash up the hill to see the "white stuff." One of those rare days is in 1985, when Santa Fe 5373 West cruised through Blue Cut, named for the blue-gray colored rocks along Cajon Creek. Blue Cut also features one of Cajon's best-known Route 66 photo locations, as illustrated by railfans in 1989.

Left: DDA40X at speed
Above: Santa Fe at Blue Cut
Right: Railfans at Blue Cut
Far right: El Cajon Motel sign

ajon's railroading tradition began with Santa Fe's predecessor California Southern in 1885, and expanded to include Union Pacific in 1905; the third railroad arrived in 1967 when Southern Pacific completed its "Palmdale Cutoff" line. Mergers have reduced the "big three" to just two—BNSF and UP—but up to 100 trains a day now cross the mountain pass. One of those trains is seen near Blue Cut in a panoramic view of the railroad and four-lane Route 66, although only two lanes are active through the pass. Just out of camera range is an old Federal migrant camp used in the 1930s to provide a safe haven for Dust Bowl emigrants, who faced harassment from locals.

Route 66 ends at Cajon Station, although a brief portion extends west from the Highway 138 interchange. Beyond that, much of the highway to Victorville is covered by the lanes of Interstate 15. One notable fragment survives as a forest service road that ducks under the rail lines. BNSF No. 1121 is crossing over this section of "dirt 66" as it helps a doublestack container train down Cajon's south track.

Far left: AT&SF bridge sign
Left: BNSF at old 66 crossing
Above: Four lanes and eastbound stacks
Right: Painted shield, Keenbrook

ORO GRANDE / HODGE

Past Cajon Summit, we descend into the great Mojave Desert, which is rapidly civilizing along its western edges thanks to rampant development in the cities of Hesperia and Victorville. It's past Victorville and the Mojave Narrows that we begin to feel the remoteness of the desert, a place where the Old West doesn't feel so ancient.

Adding to this feeling is the eccentric character of the people who live in wide-open spaces. The Bottle Tree Ranch near Helendale—an orchard of glass artistry created by Elmer Long—entertains Route 66 travelers, while at Oro Grande a stern sign beside an old Plymouth diesel draws a line in the sand for would-be trespassers. At Hodge, the "Two Sixes Company" ranch sign perfectly frames the meeting of BNSF and UP trains, their combined seven diesels sporting a rainbow of color in a sea of sagebrush.

Left: Meet at Two Sixes Co.
Top right: Warning sign, Oro Grande
Right: Bottle Ranch

BARSTOW

Barstow is a railroad town, a Santa Fe town to be specific, and it's not just because of the sprawling classification yard that dominates the first view of the city. Generations of Santa Fe men and women have called this desert junction home, and 10 years after the BNSF merger, their loyalty still runs deep. A drive down Route 66 (Main Street) reveals Santa Fe logos on storefronts, motels, restaurants, and even a McDonald's complex outfitted with passenger coaches and cabooses.

The restored Harvey House station and hotel—Casa Del Desierto, which means "House of the Desert"—is home to the Route 66 Mother Road Museum and the Western America Rail Museum. Both are fine museums, but the 1911 building needs a major tenant to ensure it doesn't fall back into disrepair. The second floor is quiet, except during tours and the occasional visit from supporters like Debra Hodkin, who manages the Mother Road museum.

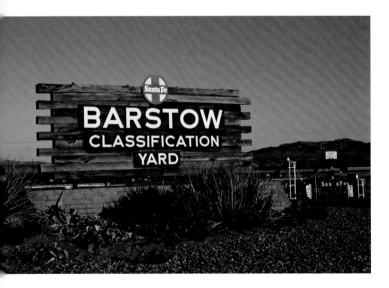

Clockwise from top left:
Santa Fe–66 mural
Restored Harvey House
Debra Hodkin
Yard entrance

anta Fe's presence grew exponentially after the 1976 opening of the new classification yard, and much of Barstow's rail activity moved to the west end. The land-mark diesel shop with its billboard "SANTA FE RAILWAY" lettering closed in 1989, moving to a modern facility west of the hump yard. Yard switchers still work at East Barstow, but it's a far cry from the days when Harvey guests gazed at a beehive of activity. For a few minutes each evening, Amtrak's *Southwest Chief* relives the days when Hi-level *El Capitans* stopped at Casa Del Desierto, but when the east-bound train departs, silence reclaims the night.

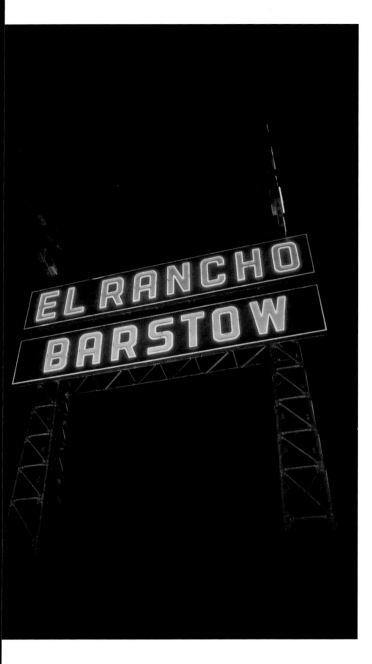

Vintage motels along Route 66 still welcome travelers in the city's historic downtown, such as the Route 66 Motel and the El Rancho, a longtime motor court. Built with ties from the Tonopah & Tidewater Railroad, the El Rancho's neon tower once beckoned weary Route 66 drivers, but the neon has since gone cold. Some consider Barstow the last civilized stop before the true desert begins—160 miles lie between here and Needles—so it's time to set out across the Mojave. The towns of Ludlow, Amboy, and Goffs await . . . don't forget the icewater.

Top left: Diesel shops
Left: Amtrak *Southwest Chief*
Above: El Rancho neon
Right: Motel row

Above: Desert Market, Daggett
Left: Eastbound at dusk

DAGGETT

Shadows grow long on the picturesque Desert Market at Daggett, a tiny town eight miles east of Barstow. Just visible in the distant mountains is Calico ghost town, one of the last surviving mining towns that once littered the Mojave. Despite its size, Daggett is a key rail junction between BNSF and Union Pacific, as part of a 1905 trackage rights deal that allowed UP trains to use the former Santa Fe from here to Riverside Junction, a distance of just over 100 miles. BNSF trains have no need to slow for the junction, so they blast through the Route 66 town at speeds up to 79 miles an hour. One of those eastbounds is seen racing under Daggett's signal bridge at dusk, the lights of Barstow barely visible in the distance.

It's a long, straight tangent from Daggett to New-berry Springs. Along the way, several desert dwellers use retired Santa Fe refrigerator cars as a creative way to beat the searing heat. The Bagdad Cafe, made famous by an independent film of the same name, is a favorite of locals, though the actual site of Bagdad is over 30 miles away.

Above: Bagdad Cafe
Left: AT&SF refrigerator car

LUDLOW

The desert communities originally began as water stops for Santa Fe's steam locomotives—a crucial role year-round, but especially during the summer months. Other towns benefited from nearby mining claims, and the small railroads that sprang up to exploit them. Nowhere was this best illustrated than in the boom town of Ludlow, the southern base of operations for the grandly named Tonopah & Tidewater and the northern end of the smaller Ludlow & Southern. The T&T ran north to gold mines in Tonopah and Goldfield in Nevada, as well as to a borax mine in Death Valley. With Santa Fe as its connection to the outside world, Ludlow became the T&T's headquarters, with engine and car shops, a station, offices, and a sweeping balloon track that circled the town. From the south, the eight-mile Ludlow & Southern swung in from the Rochester area and its "Bagdad" mine.

The Ludlow & Southern survived until 1916; the T&T ceased its Ludlow operations in 1933, lasting just seven more years before the railroad quit. The grade of the old T&T mainline is visible above the four Warbonnets leading a stack train into the hills west of town on a spring afternoon. The "new" Ludlow that sprang up around Route 66 is at left.

Drivers on I-40 see Ludlow only as a place to stop for high-priced gas, or buy ice cream at what may be the best-located Dairy Queen restaurant in all California. But the ghosts of Ludlow's past are easy to find—in the crumbling Ludlow Cafe, and in the concrete engine pits that were used to service the T&T's steam fleet. The Ludlow cemetery lies on the south side of the BNSF mainlines, yet only a handful of marble headstones preserve the memory of those who have passed into history. The rest live on as crooked wooden crosses, with names too faint to be read.

Left: Ludlow Cafe
Center: Ludlow Cemetery
Above: T&T engine pits
Right: Warbonnets leaving town

udlow's oldest structures are slowly giving way to time: much of the 1908 Murphy Bros. Mercantile Store collapsed in an earthquake. But the railroad is very much alive. The Needles Subdivision hosts a constant procession of trains led by state-of-the-art locomotives, carrying containers, truck trailers, grain, and assorted freight through a topography of basins and mountain ranges. BNSF's physical plant is equally impressive, with heavy welded rail and modern signaling that has replaced the former Santa Fe sentinels, like those that once stood beside the Route 66 crossing east of Ludlow.

But on rare occasions, Santa Fe's history becomes alive again.

Like a mirage on a hazy summer evening, AT&SF No. 3751 steams toward Ludlow with a matching train of vintage passenger coaches and domes. The restored 4-8-4, joined by two Amtrak diesels as "protection" power, is leading a 13-car excursion to Arizona for a National Railway Historical Society convention. As the golden train curves north into the Ludlow hills, a westbound stack train enters the closest curve in a rolling meet, the Warbonnet GE and the 1927 Northern dimming their headlights as they rush past each other. One wonders if the engineer of the BNSF train is rubbing his eyes in wonder at the sight . . . sometimes it's best to not question the mirage, and just enjoy it.

Above: Signals at twilight
Left: Murphy Bros. store, 1989
Opposite: NRHS excursion near Ludlow

Following pages: BNSF diesels pass
3751 excursion

Left: Rainbow power near Klondike
Below: BNSF rollby
Right: Corvette and westbound

DESERT COLORS

Some Mojave visitors see it as a bland region, but plenty of color can be found along Route 66 as it parallels the Needles Subdivision from Ludlow to Amboy. The view from Santa Fe No. 917 contrasts with the diesels of a passing BNSF eastbound, while a rainbow of paint schemes decorates a westbound as it negotiates Klondike Curve.

Buz and Tod of *Route 66* television fame would gape in wonder at the powerful Corvettes that now streak along the old highway, pacing a westbound led by Santa Fe and BNSF diesels and framed by a spectacular thunderhead. It's monsoon season in the Mojave, and soon the desert will be pounded with downpours, lightning, and flash floods. Get your kicks, indeed!

AMBOY

Roy's Cafe in Amboy was a desert oasis for Route 66 travelers for more than six decades. In 1938 Roy Crowl opened a service station to serve the parade of migrants escaping the Dust Bowl, and business was so good that long lines of cars often trailed out into the highway. So Roy, joined by son-in-law Buster Burris, opened a cafe to feed the waiting motorists. The number of stranded drivers grew with the tourism boom following World War II, and Roy and Buster added a motel. The atomic-age neon sign went up in 1958.

By 1993, as Santa Fe No. 821 raced west by the old motel and diner, Amboy was on life support, its supply of customers cut off by the interstate. Buster, its crusty "mayor"—seen riding a Santa Fe dome car on a 1990 Rail Cycle train—eventually sold his beloved outpost before passing away in 2000. It's now owned by Albert Okura, owner of a Southern California fast food chain, who bought the town and is steadily restoring the landmark diner and motel cottages. Nearby stands Amboy Crater, a stark reminder of the volcanic age that formed this Mars-like terrain.

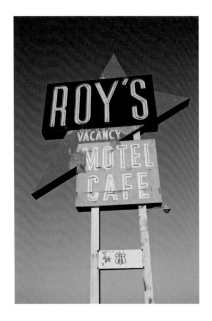

Left: Roy's sign
Below left: Buster Burris
Below: Amboy Crater
Right: Santa Fe and Roy's Cafe

CADIZ / ESSEX / GOFFS

Starting at Amboy, the midpoint between Barstow and Needles, the Southern Pacific named its stations in alphabetical order as it built east: Bristol, Cadiz, Danby, Essex, Fenner, Goffs, Homer, Ibex (now Ibis), and Java. A few new names have since been added by Santa Fe and later BNSF, but the "Alphabet Route" is still intact. Alphabets of a different kind can be found along Route 66 near Cadiz, usually spelling out names, profound phrases, and pledges of undying love. At Essex, the post-1951 alignment of Route 66 crosses over the railroad and takes a more direct route to Needles. The overpass makes a fine vantage point for train photos, and in 1992 the bridge was covered with fans snapping pictures of Santa Fe No. 3751 as she steamed east with an Employee Appreciation Special to Chicago.

Goffs Road offers a drive along the pre-1931 section of Route 66. At Goffs, a restored 1912 schoolhouse anchors a sprawling museum that includes relics from both the road and railroad. A replica of Santa Fe's Goffs passenger depot is nearing completion at the museum site.

Left: Santa Fe employee special
Top right: Route 66 rocks
Right: Relics at Goffs

Far left: Welcome wagon
Left: El Garces detail
Below: Caboose and museum train
Right: BNSF and Harvey House

NEEDLES

The welcome wagon is out for Route 66 tourists at Needles, once ground zero for the Atlantic & Pacific's turf wars with Southern Pacific. Originally called "The Needles" because of the spiky mountains along the Colorado River, the town is working to restore its glory years as a railroad and Route 66 town. Central to this effort is the long-awaited restoration of Needles' dormant Harvey House, the El Garces. Renovation has already begun thanks to millions of dollars in federal and state grants, and fifty hotel rooms and a restaurant are planned; if all goes smoothly, the resort will open in December 2008, exactly 100 years after its grand opening.

Needles is also a longtime crew-change point where the railroad's Needles and Seligman subdivisions meet. Santa Fe's red cabooses were once part of the crew change ritual, like No. 581 seen beside a "museum train" of historic locomotives bound for the California State Railroad Museum in Sacramento. In modern times, the crew of a BNSF "earthworm" grain train is preparing to end their run across the desert as they pass a westbound container train with a fresh crew. The El Garces can be seen beside Front Street, the original alignment of Route 66.

COLORADO RIVER

The mountains that gave Needles its name provide a fearsome backdrop to BNSF and Santa Fe diesels as they cross the Colorado River on the deck bridge built by Santa Fe in 1945. This is the third bridge used by the railroad to cross the river. The first was several miles north, but frequently plagued by washouts. Santa Fe built its higher Red Rock Bridge in 1890, but as trains became longer and heavier the railroad retired the cantilever in favor of the current span. The Red Rock Bridge was converted to Route 66 use, but was bypassed upon Interstate 40's arrival and later dismantled.

Near the Red Rock abutments, a stone billboard once greeted Route 66 travelers with the slogan, "Breathe deeply folks, soon you'll be in Arizona." Today it welcomes nostalgia tourists and points them to the Topock exit, where new roadside discoveries await on the road to Kingman.

Before crossing the Colorado via I-40, the Park Moabi exit leads to the old pavement that gave drivers their first look at the California desert. Looking west, a freight cruises above Route 66 led by Norfolk Southern No. 2732, a visiting SD70M-2 from the East Coast . . . another traveler following the Mother Road into the Golden State.

Left: The Needles
Above: Park Moabi
Right: Arizona welcome sign

Arizona

Northern Arizona is the one state where Route 66 and the former Santa Fe Railway are constant companions from end to end. In fewer than 400 miles, the road and railroad climb through deserts, canyons, and forests, before crossing the 7,354-foot Arizona Divide . . . then leave Flagstaff and the mountains behind to sprint east through the Petrified Forest and Painted Desert before reaching the New Mexico border at Lupton.

Along the way, they also thread Kingman and Crozier canyons, pass through the largest stand of Ponderosa Pines in the country, and whisk through a chain of historic towns, each with their own unique personality: Kingman, Seligman, Ash Fork, Williams, Winslow, and Holbrook. Even fast-growing Flagstaff, nestled at the foot of the San Francisco Peaks, holds firmly to its railroad and highway history.

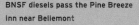

BNSF diesels pass the Pine Breeze Inn near Bellemont

This is the state where the Mother Road was reborn, and where the longest unbroken section of the highway can still be driven—159 miles from the Colorado River to just west of Ash Fork. From a railfan's perspective, only New Mexico is as closely tied to the heritage of the Santa Fe Railway and its successor BNSF. The legacy of steel and asphalt can be found in every town, but it's especially visible in places like Bellemont, high in the Kaibab National Forest, where a BNSF trailer train passes silent gas pumps at the old Pine Breeze Inn.

Arizona may be home to the grandest of all canyons, but the state offers so much more. Let's follow Chico's railroad through this exciting land; chances are good that a fast train will be at our side.

TOPOCK / YUCCA

Exhaust trailing into the hot sky, BNSF 7723 East is barely a quarter mile into Arizona as it rounds the big curve at Topock on the east side of the Colorado River. Behind the colorful GE diesels is the Trails Arch Bridge, the original highway span that opened in 1916, ten years before Route 66 existed. It carries a pipeline now, but is no less impressive. The old highway is here too; it begins beside the river and ducks under the railroad to head northeast to Oatman and navigate treacherous Sitgreaves Pass to Kingman. The railroad parallels the post-1952 route, largely replaced by I-40.

Yucca, an old Santa Fe water stop, also reveals remnants of Route 66. A wooden box car rests under budding thunderclouds, while signs for a Whiting Bros. gas station and motel stand against a dramatic sky. Now extinct, the chain was once synonymous with the Mother Road; only a handful of its red and yellow structures remain.

Left: Eastbound with Trails Arch Bridge
Right: Box car, Yucca
Below: Whiting Bros. ruins, Yucca

KINGMAN

With a survey crew of 20 men and a few mules, Lewis Kingman established the route of the Atlantic & Pacific's Western Division across Arizona, much of which is still followed by BNSF. In spring 1880, Kingman was Santa Fe's locating engineer; Chief Engineer Henry Holbrook instructed him to head directly to the Colorado River and establish an eastward route up the steep Arizona Divide. Fifty-five miles from the river a township was founded, naming itself Kingman in 1882. By then Lewis Kingman had succeeded Holbrook as chief engineer, but left the A&P three days after the railroad arrived in his namesake town.

Today's Kingman may not be a metropolis, but its downtown is filled with character and history. Route 66 is named Andy Devine Boulevard, in honor of the Hollywood actor who grew up here. With the renaissance of Route 66 tourism in Mohave County (Arizona spells it with an "h"), the city has embraced both its Mother Road and railroad heritage. A 1907-built power plant is now a Route 66 museum and visitor's center, and across the street sits Santa Fe 4-8-4 No. 3759, donated in 1956.

Rolling past Kingman's landmark water tanks, an eastbound BNSF train makes a colorful sight thanks to the presence of Santa Fe No. 631, a General Electric Dash 9-44CW still wearing its obsolete Warbonnet colors. In Locomotive Park, No. 3759 slumbers near a historic road sign. In 2002, celebrity sister No. 3751 paused beside the 1907 depot en route to Williams.

Warbonnet, downtown Kingman

Above: No. 3751, Kingman depot

Right: Locomotive Park

East of Kingman, Route 66 and the old Santa Fe set off for Seligman on what may be the country's best-preserved section of the highway—nearly 90 miles of pristine, two-lane asphalt. The interstate is far from sight, taking travelers to a time when the railroad was a driver's only companion. Looking back at Kingman in twilight, the town resembles the runway lights of an airport, the descent via Route 66 more like a final approach. In the distance, the headlight of an eastbound BNSF train keeps pace with a parade of oncoming cars, their lights forming a chain that will soon break the calm of a warm summer's evening.

West of town is Kingman Canyon, one of the railroad's most iconic locations. In Santa Fe days, three shiny Warbonnets lead a train of California-bound containers through the canyon. This view reveals layers of history: No. 839 is using the original 1883 mainline, while the photographer is standing near the 1923-built second track. The original section of Route 66 is visible beside the locomotives, while the modern version is on the distant hillside. One wonders what Lewis Kingman would think if he had seen the sleek Santa Fe streamliners that were once so synonymous with the Southwest . . . or the BNSF container trains that snake in and out of his namesake town using the same routes he established over 125 years ago.

East Kingman at dusk

Following pages: Kingman Canyon

CROZIER CANYON

Twenty-six miles east of Kingman, the Hackberry General Store delivers a colorful assortment of photo opportunities. Santa Fe and Route 66 signs share wall space, while vintage gas pumps, sedans, and a 1956 Corvette greet travelers who stop for snacks and souvenirs. Hackberry marks the entrance to Crozier Canyon, where Santa Fe No. 5026 and four more blue units pass an eastbound counterpart in 1993. The A&P first built through Crozier in 1883, moving to a higher shelf when the original route was washed away by floods. Today's BNSF hugs the west side of Truxton Wash at the foot of Route 66; this portion of the highway was the last to be paved, around 1937. Few roadside relics survive from the days when 66 and the *Chief* trains hosted vacationers through the canyon, but the Chief's Motel sign at Valentine is a notable exception. Until the town dried up, the Valentine post office was a popular place to mail cards and letters on February 14!

Opposite: Crozier Canyon
Left: Signs at Hackberry
Below left: Chief's Motel near Valentine
Below: Hackberry General Store

AUBREY VALLEY

ast Truxton, the Mother Road follows the BNSF mainlines through the Hualapai Native American Reservation, passing Peach Springs and stealing a glance at the Grand Canyon's west rim before emerging into the wide Aubrey Valley. Big skies and golden fields dwarf the passing of an eastbound BNSF freight with older diesels, as it rolls through a big curve at Audley on a beautiful summer afternoon. Santa Fe inexplicably renamed Aubrey to Audley in the early 1900s, to avoid a supposed conflict elsewhere on the railroad.

No matter which name you use, it's hard to ignore a nearby Arizona attraction: the Grand Canyon Caverns, with spectacular cave tours that take tourists 21 stories below the surface . . . all guarded by a bloodthirsty Allosaurus at the Caverns' entrance. At Chino Point, the road and railroad squeeze around the Aubrey Cliffs and begin their descent to Seligman, a former Santa Fe division point and the birthplace of the modern Route 66 renaissance. A visit is in order . . . but first let's enjoy the sight of BNSF 5444 East as the freight climbs out of town under monsoonal skies.

Above: Westbound leaving Seligman
Left: Grand Canyon Caverns
Right: Eastbound at Audley

Angel Delgadillo

SELIGMAN

Angel Delgadillo strides onto the crumbling brick platform of the Havasu Hotel in Seligman, a former crew change point for Santa Fe's Seligman and Winslow Districts. He surveys the old Harvey House, built in 1905 with an unusual English Tudor motif, now succumbing to age and neglect. A BNSF signboard is the lone clue to the building's owner, which in 2007 announced plans to tear down the structure. Preservation groups mobilized, but funding and resources were slim; demolition began in spring 2008.

Angel is Seligman's part-time barber and its most famous resident. A warm man with a big smile and untiring energy, he helped launch the Historic Route 66 Association of Arizona, which renewed interest in the old road and triggered a wave of revivals from Chicago to Los Angeles.

Named after investment banker Jesse Seligman, this is where the worlds of Route 66 and the Santa Fe Railway

are joined the closest, their souls intertwined. Other towns tell similar stories, but Seligman best symbolizes the rise, decline, and rebirth of the road and railroad.

Santa Fe's famed streamliners vanished in 1971, discarded with the rise of interstates and air travel. Seligman's turn for obsolescence came on September 22, 1978, when Interstate 40 opened a mile away. In a single day, thousands of cars vanished from the main drag. But that was only the first strike of a cruel, one-two punch. In 1985, Santa Fe bypassed the town as a crew change point. As devastating as the loss of Route 66 was, the loss of the town's rail population was far worse.

"We knew them all by name," explains Angel, whose father was a machinist for Santa Fe before becoming a barber. "This was their home away from home . . . they ate at our restaurants, they drank at our bars. They were always at the fundraisers at our schools and churches."

Since crews would lay over 24 hours between runs, many lived in "shacks," small structures outfitted with basic lights and utilities. The Delgadillos rented out rooms to Santa Fe men, and after Angel opened his barbershop in 1950 he'd give as many as five haircuts a day to railroaders.

"We had a built-in, year round economy," he notes. "When we were bypassed by the interstate it hurt the restaurants, the gas stations, the motels . . . but when the railroad men left, that's when it hurt everyone. In that ten-year period after I-40 bypassed us and then Santa Fe, you couldn't give your property away."

Happily, Seligman has returned to prosperity. The Delgadillo barbershop—now a Route 66 gift center— serves more visitors than ever, and Angel still gives the occasional haircut via his 1926 chair. He points out that international visitors make up most of his tourist trade. "They know the value of history, and that's what we helped preserve—a little bit of history."

Left: Angel's barber shop
Right: Seligman welcome sign

On the Havasu Hotel's south side, it's a racetrack of railroading. Freight trains used to stop at the old Harvey House, but now they blur past like Santa Fe No. 136, her colors evoking the spirits of *Chiefs* long gone. Looking through the Harvey House's pillars, a modern heir —Amtrak's *Southwest Chief*—rushes by in summer 2004, just months before the building was fenced in hopes of eventual restoration.

On the north side, Route 66 cruises through eclectic charm. The best show in town is the Snow Cap restaurant. Juan Delgadillo, Angel's late brother, made the diner infamous with zany antics like offering customers "dead chicken" and "used" straws and napkins. Juan's comic legacy lives on through his family, who continues the Snow Cap tradition, and through "Juan's Garden," a quirky assortment of Santa Fe and highway memorabilia. Nearby, the manequins of The Rusty Bolt store recreate the 1950s with plastic perfection. Seligman is a Route 66 town that makes its own rules—and the zanier, the better.

Right: Seligman Harvey House
Above: Amtrak train No. 4

From left:
Snow Cap
Waitress, Rusty Bolt
Snow Cap sign

Clockwise, from above:
Flagstone
Water tank, Ash Fork
Route 66 Diner

ASH FORK / WILLIAMS

Williams Flyover

East of Seligman is Crookton, the west end of a 44-mile, $17.8 million line relocation that Santa Fe completed in 1960. East of the Route 66 overpass, the relocated mainlines bear northeast and complete a series of sweeping curves before rejoining the original route past Williams. Nineteen miles of twisting track were removed between Crookton and Ash Fork. The latter was once the site of a key junction between the original main and Santa Fe's route to Phoenix. Today, westbound trains simply turn south at Ash Fork and an empty railroad grade continues west, visible from 66 and I-40.

Ash Fork struggled after Santa Fe's departure and the interstate's arrival. Yet it endures, thanks to ranching, tourism, and its reputation as the "Flagstone Capital of the World." Santa Fe relics remain, most notably the water tank beside westbound 66.

Beyond Ash Fork, the original track ascends forested table lands before entering downtown Williams. The newer line circles around town, crossing over the Grand Canyon Railway, a former Santa Fe branch. The flyover presents all kinds of opportunities to photograph different generations of railroading, especially when the tourist railroad poses 2-8-2 No. 4960 and train below the BNSF line. The Phoenix line parallels Route 66 and Williams' charming downtown district. Coasting by at a leisurely pace, an eastbound freight barely warrants a glance from Route 66 Diner waitress Carol Howard while she chats with tourists Robbie Gould and Belinda McConnell.

WILLIAMS

The sight of Grand Canyon Railway No. 18 returning to Williams on a fall evening reflects the revival of not only a Route 66 town, but the Arizona steam experience. The tourist railroad revitalized this mountain town, whose fortunes have risen and fallen since the Atlantic & Pacific arrived in 1882. Santa Fe's Grand Canyon branch was completed in 1901; a Fred Harvey hotel, the Fray Marcos, opened in 1908. Over the decades, Williams billed itself as the "Gateway to the Grand Canyon," and millions of passengers rode Santa Fe trains to the national park. The last passenger train stopped at the Grand Canyon in 1968 and AT&SF soon abandoned the line. Eventually the town became home to the last commissioned section of Route 66. That distinction ended on October 13, 1984, when the final leg of Interstate 40 opened and the 66 signs came down.

Above: Harvey House
Right: Readying No. 18

Above: Williams Flyer

The town spiraled into decline, but entrepreneurs Max and Thelma Biegert purchased the Grand Canyon branch just as scrap crews were beginning to dismantle it. On a cold Friday evening in September 1989, the restored Fray Marcos was once again surrounded by celebrations, even as crews worked around the clock to ready 2-8-0 No. 18 for the Grand Canyon Railway's "re-inaugural" voyage. On September 17—exactly 88 years after Santa Fe ran its first train to the canyon—the VIP special steamed to the South Rim Village, arriving beside the Harvey-built El Tovar hotel. Eighteen years later, about 220,000 people a year ride the rails to one of America's greatest wonders.

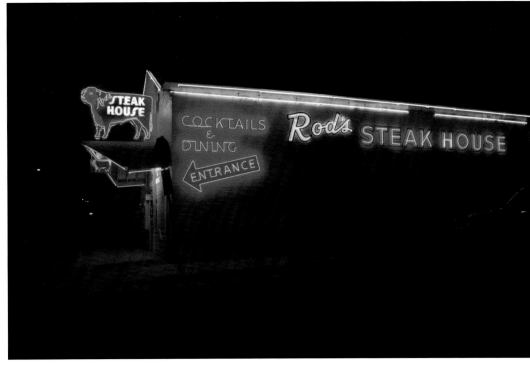

WILLIAMS / MAINE

Williams offers more than just the Grand Canyon Railway, of course. Shops, retro diners, and charming motels line Route 66 as it splits into one-way streets through the downtown area. BNSF's relocated "Transcon" curves around town, so residents are spared the constant activity of a high-density railroad. East of town, trains glide above Route 66 on a bridge that still bears Santa Fe's circle-and-cross logo and billboard lettering. Barely visible are the letters that once read, "It's fun to ride . . ."

Rod's Steak House, opened by Rod Graves in 1946, is a local institution with its signature steer, who seems right at home resting beside a Santa Fe signpost. At night, Rod's neon glows like a beacon for hungry travelers . . . not unlike the old AT&SF signal bridges that guided passing trains at Maine, a railroad point in the Kaibab National Forest between Williams and Flagstaff.

Opposite: East Williams bridge
Above left: Maine signals and moon
Above: Steak house neon
Left: Signs and Rod's menus, Williams

FLAGSTAFF

Entering Flagstaff, Route 66 is a bustling four-lane highway that follows the BNSF mainlines through the city's historic downtown. The city's name can be traced back to July 4, 1876, when the fledgling town hung their American flag on a tall tree stripped of its branches. The A&P arrived in summer 1882, and the town immediately swelled in population. The first "depot" was nothing more than two box cars parked on a side track, hardly the stuff of civic pride. A structure followed, but promptly burned down in July 1889. A stone replacement was succeeded by a Tudor Revival–style station in 1926, which remains unlike any other depot in Arizona. The stone depot became Santa Fe's freight station, and is still used today by BNSF. The distinctive passenger station serves as both an Amtrak stop and a visitor's center, sandwiched between the road and railroad.

The entire scene is visible from the Lowell Observatory on nearby Mars Hill, as a westbound rolls through downtown with a string of colorful containers. Route 66 motels have always been plagued by the constant blare of horns from passing trains—enough that some establishments tout "No Railroad Noise" on their marquees. That "noise" is about to vanish, however, thanks to a track relocation project east of the downtown district. Soon, all Route 66 tourists will hear is the city's night life along this vibrant section of the Mother Road.

Above: Freight house

Right: Passenger depot

Left: Downtown Flagstaff
Above: "No Rail Road Noise"

WINONA / TWIN ARROWS

"Don't forget Winona," sang Bobby Troup, but someone neglected to tell the Santa Fe. The railroad named this place Darling, and that's what the classic signpost reads on a stormy 2004 afternoon. Not much remains of the actual Winona, except a trading post and gas station at Exit 211 beside Interstate 40. Regardless, Winona offers a panoramic view of the San Francisco Peaks above Flagstaff and the surrounding Coconino National Forest. On a crisp 1993 morning, a "Pepsi-Can" GE leads Amtrak train No. 4, the eastbound *Southwest Chief*, under the Route 66 overpass, a popular photo location. At right, the pre-1947 route can be seen winding through the pines to Flagstaff.

Heading east from Winona, the forest gradually opens up to wide plains and wider skies. I-40 covers much of the old highway, while the railroad drifts farther north and crosses canyons Padre and Diablo. Tourist towns like Twin Arrows and Two Guns litter the occasional interstate exit, but all that remains are the ruins of gas stations, roadside zoos, concrete bridges, and a pair of oversize red and yellow arrows.

Left: *Southwest Chief* **at Winona**
Below: **Twin Arrows**
Right: **AT&SF signpost**

Left: Winslow "Eagles" corner
Below: La Posada
Right: BNSF trains at West Winslow

WINSLOW

How deeply has the Eagles' recording of "Take it Easy" influenced roadside America? Look no farther than downtown Winslow. "Standing on the corner in Winslow, Arizona" has drawn generations of fans here ever since Glenn Frey sang those lyrics. The town's "official" corner is located at Second Street (Route 66) and Kinsley Street, not far from the BNSF yard. Step outside on a summer's evening, and you'll hear Frey's voice echoing from the surrounding gift shops.

Winslow received its rail connection to the world in 1881; west of town, A&P track crews reached the midway point between the Rio Grande and Colorado rivers. With such a strategic location, the town became a major terminal and crew change point, complete with locomotive and car shops. Today's westbound trains leave the Gallup Subdivision here and enter the Seligman Subdivision. On a hot June 2007 afternoon, brand-new BNSF No. 7551 leaves Winslow for the Arizona Divide; in the distance, two westbounds can be seen entering the yard limits.

Not to be missed is the La Posada, the final Harvey House designed by Mary Colter, architect and designer for the Fred Harvey Company. Beautifully restored to its 1929 elegance, the "Resting Place" offers a first-class hotel experience, fine dining in the Turquoise Room restaurant, and daily train service by the *Southwest Chief*.

JACKRABBIT / HOLBROOK

E n route to Holbrook, a stop is required at the Jackrabbit, an iconic Route 66 trading post near the town of Joseph City. Announced for miles by yellow signs with black silhouettes of its namesake mascot, travelers are greeted by an immense "HERE IT IS" sign next to the BNSF mainlines. An eastbound grain train rolls by in 2005, making a fine sight in early morning light; before leaving, let's take a photo atop the fiberglass jackrabbit beside the trading post.

Home of the infamous Bucket of Blood saloon, the Atlantic & Pacific entered Holbrook in September 1881; three years later, Fred Harvey established one of his first Harvey House restaurants in five box cars near the depot. It wasn't much on the outside, but inside guests found an oasis of civility. In 1888 a raging fire destroyed most of the town, but Harvey's box car restaurant escaped damage. The citizens rebuilt, beginning with a new stone depot that still stands near the junction of Route 66 and Navajo Boulevard. In Santa Fe's "Super Fleet" era, an eastbound blasts through downtown Holbrook with a shiny Warbonnet quintet.

Opposite: Santa Fe eastbound, Holbrook　　**Top left: Jackrabbit Trading Post**
Top right: Fiberglass jackrabbit
Above: Rainbow Rock Shop

Left: Wigwam Motel, Holbrook
Below: Warbonnet and wigwams
Right: Motel office at dusk

TEEPEES

Sleep in a Wigwam. These four words have sent gener-ations of kids into a frenzy, pleading with their parents to stay the night in a concrete teepee. One of three remaining teepee-styled motels in the country, Holbrook's Wigwam Motel was opened by Chester Lewis in 1950, patterned after a similar establishment in Kentucky. The wigwams were refurbished in 1988, and the interiors feature polished wood, a quaint bed, and more space than one would expect. Thanks to nostalgia tourism, the wigwams have become the hottest teepees on the high-way, and routinely sell out during the summer months. After sunset, they take on a surreal beauty in the gather-ing darkness.

The only chiefs to be found in Holbrook are of the steel-wheeled variety, such as BNSF No. 558 switching the small yard in 2004. Only along Route 66 could a photographer find a locomotive wearing a headdress near a village of concrete wigwams.

HOLBROOK / ADAMANA

Another Holbrook attraction—though nothing that would appear in a Chamber of Commerce brochure—is the Apache Railway, a 38-mile shortline that runs from Snowflake north to the BNSF connection at Holbrook. With a locomotive fleet built by the defunct Alco Locomotive Company, the Apache is a dream come true for diesel fans. On a spectacular October afternoon, a trio of C420s—Nos. 82, 83, and 81, all built between 1964 and 1967—pull their southbound train out of town, an ear-rattling experience of sight and sound. These aren't the only dinosaurs in Holbrook, however; the petrified wood shop east of town offers an assortment of its own beasts.

Opposite: Apache Railway and
roadside dinosaurs

Left: Amtrak at Adamana
Below: Stewart's Petrified Wood

New Mexico is only 70 miles east of Holbrook, and the road and railroad will pass through Petrified Forest National Park and Navajo Native American land. The *Southwest Chief* speeds through the park near the old station of Adamana, an exotic land of mesas instantly branding the Southwest setting. Several miles north, cross-country travelers interrupted their Route 66 vacation for a detour to see the fields of prehistoric wood. For those that can't make a side trip, plenty of roadside tourist traps exist to entice motorists with petrified souvenirs.

ADAMANA / QUERINO / LUPTON

The Santa Fe name survives in the unlikeliest of places . . . such as this road sign on Petrified Forest Road, above a passing westbound that sports two variations of the BNSF design. A day of train-watching from this over-pass nets a surprising variety of trains and camera angles—but New Mexico is calling, and it's time to leap back onto I-40. Route 66 exists only in fragments at this end of the state, so it's easiest to drive the interstate and exit onto frontage roads only when a photo simply must be captured. One of those moments is a retreating thunderstorm seen from Querino, as I-40 traffic and the passage of an eastbound freight border the electric sky. Dramatic cliffs and Native American shops line the state border town of Lupton, and in moments we'll enter the Land of Enchantment.

Above: Chief Yellowhorse, Lupton
Left: BNSF, Petrified Forest Road
Right: Lightning storm, Querino

New Mexico

Layers of history follow Route 66 and the old Santa Fe through New Mexico, layers such as those found in spectacular Mesa Gigante, towering above a westbound BNSF container train in 2007. At the western end of the state, trains and tourists enter the Land of Enchantment via the same route that Atlantic & Pacific surveyors established in 1881. Tall colorful cliffs border Route 66, the railroad, and Interstate 40 as the ribbons of steel and asphalt squeeze through the scenery. And the thrills don't stop upon arrival at Gallup. Red Rock State Park, once the setting for hundreds of Hollywood westerns, provides a panoramic background for 66 and the old Santa Fe as they run through towns bearing the names of Thoreau, Grants, and Cubero. Farther east lie the reservation towns of Laguna and Mesita, the home of Mesa Gigante.

Like a modern-day wagon train, a westbound rolls past Mesita.

When first commissioned in 1926, westbound Route 66 met the Santa Fe's Raton Pass mainline at Romeroville near Las Vegas (New Mexico), and together the two routes climbed 7,432-foot Glorieta Pass. They parted briefly as 66 passed through the state capital of Santa Fe—something the city's namesake railroad did only via a branch line from Lamy—and eventually rejoined to follow the Rio Grande River to Bernalillo and Albuquerque. The two routes continued south to Los Lunas, and then began their epic journey west to the Pacific Coast.

Little more than a decade after the highway's christening, progress brought significant changes to both road and railroad in New Mexico. In 1937, Route 66's "Santa Fe Loop" was replaced by a straight-arrow section between Santa Rosa and Albuquerque. Farther west, the section between Los Lunas and Correo across the Rio Puerco River was also bypassed. Following the 1995 BNSF merger, traffic on the Raton Pass mainline steadily dwindled to a shadow of its former self, in favor of the railroad's newer Belen Cutoff line and its easier grades. The pre-1937 sections of 66 endure, as does the original Glorieta Pass mainline, and they offer a scenic alternative to the interstates.

New Mexico delivers spectacle from the moment one leaves Arizona behind. It's a mystical and spiritual land, where skies feature a deeper blue and the clouds seem to reach down and touch the red mesas. Gazing at Mesa Gigante as it dwarfs a westbound container train, it's hard not to think of movie directors such as John Ford and Sergio Leone, and wonder if this is where the word "panorama" was invented.

DEFIANCE

Chief Yellowhorse's tourist traps are washed away in a sigh of exhaust from four orange BNSF diesels, accelerating across the Arizona–New Mexico border with a colorful train of stacked containers. "The Land of Sunshine" delivers a great entrance for highway travelers. Route 66 immediately makes a scenic break from the interstate, following the former Santa Fe and the Rio Puerco River between a series of mesas. The old trading posts at Manuelito are long gone, but early- and late-day lighting make for dramatic views. Afternoon shadows swallow the sentinel cliffs while an eastbound train bursts into a strip of sunlight; with backlit exhaust, the stack train appears to be pouring on the power in pursuit of a speeding pickup on old 66.

On a perfect summer morning, tourist slogans adorn a colorful billboard near Defiance, while the highway and a westbound freight skirt the heel of dramatically named "Devil's Cliff." The billboard may tout New Mexico's western neighbor, but this scene—aided by a rainbow of colors on the passing diesels—is classic Southwest spectacle. "Bring your cameras," indeed! If a tourist hasn't picked up a camera by now, the trip is already a lost cause.

Above: Eastbound at Defiance
Right: BNSF entering New Mexico

GALLUP

Gallup has the distinction of being the sole New Mexico city mentioned in Bobby Troup's anthem to the Mother Road, "Get Your Kicks." Its genesis can be traced to Atlantic & Pacific paymaster David Gallup, who located his headquarters beside the railroad's right of way. Rail crews would "go to Gallup" to get their paychecks, and in 1881 the town took his name.

Gallup's Route 66 roots run deep, and the highway follows the railroad into downtown, where a small switching yard remains. The city is a hub for numerous Native American nations—including the Navajo, Acoma, Hopi, and Zuni—and the Southwest's largest center for original Native American art. During the Santa Fe passenger years, Native American guides would ride the *Super Chief* and *El Capitan* between Gallup and Albuquerque, pointing out landmarks and sharing their culture and beliefs. Amtrak carries on this tradition with its *Southwest Chief* trains, which continue to stop at the site of the old Harvey Hotel, El Navajo, now a museum. Nearby sits a retired Santa Fe caboose, dressed with an impressive mural of the highways that crisscross the state, including Interstate 40 and Route 66.

Left: Billboard, Defiance
Below: Caboose map, Gallup

GALLUP

Reminders of the road's legacy include the delightful Route 66 sign atop the chamber of commerce building, designed by author Jerry McClanahan. Farther east is the 1937-built El Rancho Hotel, once the home for Hollywood crews filming westerns in nearby Red Rock Park. From the 1930s through the 1950s, stars like Kirk Douglas, Ronald Reagan, Katharine Hepburn, and Jackie Cooper stayed at the grand lodge with its rustic Old West interior. After years of decline, the resort was saved by fourth-generation Indian trader Armand Ortega. Today, despite the change in signage from "hotel" to "motel," the El Rancho's splendor has been preserved. The plantation-style entrance carries the slogan "Charm of Yesterday . . . Convenience of Tomorrow," and travelers who stay at the El Rancho quickly realize that it's one of the Mother Road's crown jewels.

GALLUP / CONTINENTAL DIVIDE

anta Fe's Warbonnet was a natural fit in New Mexico, where its bright red, yellow, and silver colors perfectly complemented the cliffs and spires that follow the railroad and Route 66 east from Gallup. In 1991, Santa Fe No. 120 and four sisters—the last engine a cabless "B" unit —make a vibrant display of Leland Knickerbocker's design near Red Rock State Park, visible at far right. The panoramic backdrops were no less spectacular when balanced against the railroad's old blue and yellow diesels, as illustrated by a westbound train rolling past Church Rock in that same year.

Twenty-seven miles past Gallup lies the Continental Divide, with a marker that denotes the divide separating the water drainage to the Pacific from that into the Gulf of Mexico. Nearby, a local gift shop does its best to divide highway travelers from their tourist dollars, standing under an impressive "Kodachrome sky."

Below: GP60Ms near Red Rock Park

Left: Santa Fe and Church Rock

Above: Continental Divide

PREWITT / GRANTS

Route 66 travelers are accustomed to ruins, but the sight of old box cars under the New Mexico sun are a sharp contrast to the typical remnants of cafes and motels that line the highway en route to Grants. Seen near the railroad location of West Baca, the box cars lie in various stages of distress, colors fading under a tapestry of clouds. Couplers reach out in the sand, their grasps unmet.

Ruins of "dirt 66" can also be found near Prewitt. BNSF No. 688, wearing her original Santa Fe colors, crosses a stone bridge that reveals a distant wooden trestle used by the highway's earliest alignment. A far more modern version of 66 spans today's BNSF at Grants, where state-of-the-art No. 7794 leads a piggyback train under a gathering summer storm.

Right: Warbonnet and original road
Above: Box cars' graveyard
Left: BNSF at Grants

GRANTS / LAGUNA

East of Grants, road signs reflect Route 66's current and past lives while an eastbound trailer train rolls through the high desert terrain. Highway 118 ends at this junction near I-40 exit no. 89, but Highway 124 will allow travelers to continue east on the old road—in all, 70 miles of uninterrupted Route 66 driving between the Continental Divide and Mesita. Next up is Acoma reservation land, with a peaceful trek for both the road and railroad through gentle hills, Native American pueblos, and modern-day ghost towns. McCartys falls into the latter category, with an impressive pair of Whiting Bros. signs that face the Mother Road. Only the concrete foundation remains of the chain's motor court, and the service station has crumbled into ruin.

Blink and you'll miss the tiny 66 towns of Budville and Cubero. The highway drifts far from the railroad and I-40 before the three routes converge near New Laguna. Long rows of telephone poles, now an endangered species, add trackside character to the passage of BNSF 4626 West. The rising sun glints off the three GE diesels and their train, while glass insulators on the poles seemingly light the way to California.

Above: Highway signs near Grants
Right: Whiting Bros. relics, McCartys
Opposite: Telephone pole line, Laguna

LAGUNA

Old and New Laguna are located in the heart of Laguna Pueblo land, and both towns are equally historic and picturesque. Thunderous sound envelops New Laguna as two distributed power units (DPUs) push on the rear of a coal train bound for the Defiance mine near Gallup. The nose of an eastbound trailer train waits in the distance like a mirage, its shape distorted by the helper engines' rising curtain of exhaust.

An early version of Route 66 once passed through New Laguna, now called Santa Fe Avenue. Crumbling homes don't do much to support the "new" moniker, but they add historic context to a BNSF train in November 2005. Upon rejoining newer 66, travelers arrive at the charming village of Laguna, where the 1699-built San Jose de Laguna Mission stands in sharp contrast with a cobalt blue New Mexico sky.

Left: Coal train helpers, Laguna

Top right: New Laguna ruins

Right: San Jose de Laguna Mission, Laguna Pueblo

CORREO / NINE MILE HILL

Heading to the outpost of Correo, travelers can either drive the sterile convenience of Interstate 40 or navigate one of the earliest sections of Route 66. The pre-1937 alignment joins up with the railroad in Correo—where a BNSF westbound is seen from the old highway bridge—and follows the rails to Los Lunas. West of town, the Raton Subdivision darts under the highway, having split from the busy "Transcon" mainlines at Dalies. Upon reaching Los Lunas, 66 turns north and loosely parallels the Raton line to Albuquerque.

Those seeking a faster drive can follow the post-1937 alignment from Correo, although it's largely buried under the interstate. No railroad is in sight, but near the Rio Puerco River crossing is a modern monument that rivals any of the old road's kitschy marketing gimmicks: the Route 66 Casino and Travel Center, with towering gas pumps, oversized neon arrows, and a shield-shaped entrance. Cyrus Avery would be proud.

The western approach into Albuquerque reveals one of the more dramatic sights on all of Route 66. Nestled in the Rio Grande Valley, the lights of New Mexico's largest city glitter under the Sandia Mountains. At the top of "Nine Mile Hill," 66 expands into four lanes and becomes Central Avenue as it descends into the city. West of the Rio Grande River, an iconic shield casts a neon glow over the Mother Road, announcing that we've entered a city where Route 66 is again a downtown centerpiece.

Clockwise from left:
Route 66 Casino
Westbound at Correo
Neon along Central Avenue

Opposite:
Nine Mile Hill, Albuquerque

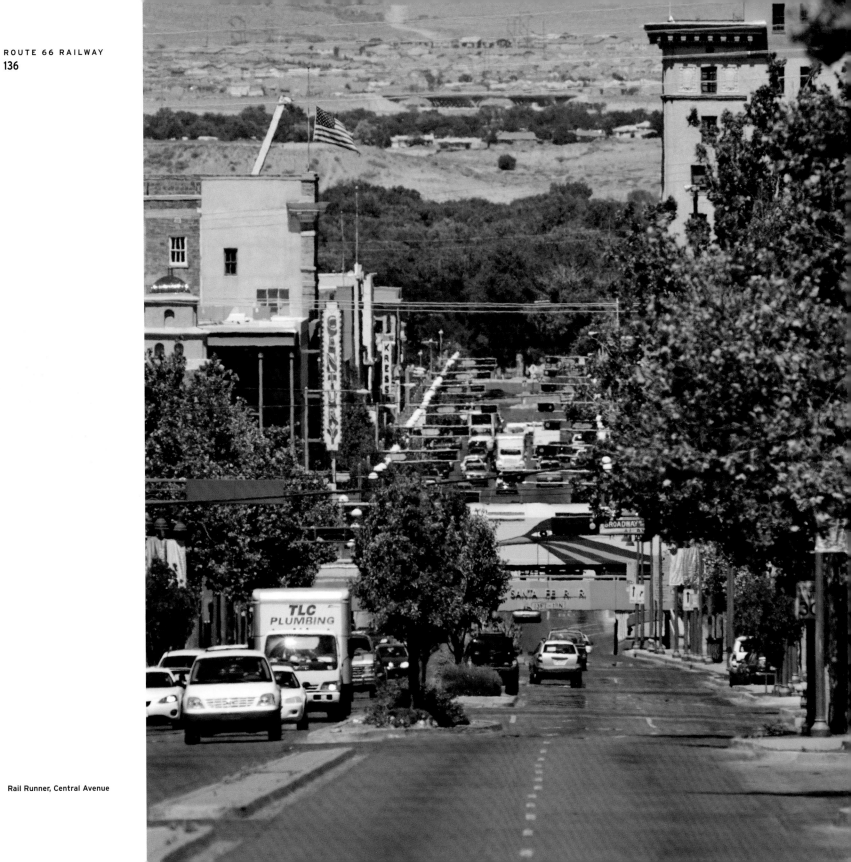

Rail Runner, Central Avenue

ALBUQUERQUE

Albuquerque was founded in 1706 as the "Villa of Alburquerque," named by acting governor don Francisco Cuervo y Valdes, who demonstrated his political savvy by inflating the population count when he announced the settlement to his superiors in Mexico. During the 300 years that followed, the city fell under United States rule and lost the extra "r." The Atlantic & Pacific arrived in 1880, building a north-south route that paralleled the Rio Grande River, but on higher ground to avoid flooding.

In 1902, Santa Fe built the Hotel Alvarado, the "jewel in its crown," and the city sprang up around it. One of Fred Harvey's most impressive establishments, the resort sported courtyards, fountains, bell towers, and served as the city's social and political center. The hotel and station complex were located beside Railroad Avenue, which was renamed Central Avenue in 1907 and became part of Route 66 in 1937.

The Rio Grande is shrouded by trees as a "Rail Runner" commuter train darts across Central Avenue, adding a splash of color on a summer 2007 morning. When the downtown drag became part of Route 66 in 1937, the underpass was built to relieve motorists from the constant activity of Santa Fe freight and passenger trains. But by the 1960s, passenger trains were on the decline and downtown began to languish. Residents moved out to the suburbs, and businesses followed them to shopping centers and malls.

The Alvarado was eventually abandoned. City leaders tried to buy the property, but they were slow to act; despite community outrage, Santa Fe bulldozed the historic hotel in 1970. The surviving station shifted to Amtrak use, and it burned to the ground in 1993.

Albuquerque's downtown is busy again following a 10-year revitalization program along Route 66. The hotel site is now home to the Alvarado Transportation Center, a city transit hub, and a Greyhound bus station that replicates the depot's architecture. Santa Fe's presence is faint, since BNSF has routed most of its trains to the southern Belen-Amarillo route. But new "Rail Runner" trains continue

Clockwise from top:
Rail Runner trains
Alvarado postcard
Downtown mural, 2007

to grow in popularity. Adorned with feathered mascots, modern MP36 diesels sprint over Route 66 several times a day en route to the nearby towns of Bernalillo and Belen. The Alvarado may be gone, but passenger trains and Route 66 have returned to Central Avenue.

Until 1937, Route 66 took a north-south path through Albuquerque, dropping down from Santa Fe. After a direct link was completed between the city and Santa Rosa (114 miles east), the highway adapted an east-west route. Motorists who drive early 66 cross the newer alignment in downtown and farther south they pass the former Santa Fe locomotive shops, which once employed up to 25 percent of the city's population. Built in the early 1920s, the towering machine and boiler shops were cathedrals of industry, but their round-the-clock activity ceased when the complex closed in the 1970s.

Galvanized by losses like the Alvarado, the city and its preservation community have saved the 27-acre site from the wrecking ball, and the vacant shops await a possible future as a transportation museum. For now they stand in silence. Railroad symbolism runs deep in a view of Santa Fe Avenue, the shop buildings, and the A&P Bar, named after the railroad that sparked this city.

Several blocks away, more roadside relics await the traveler. A revitalized Central Avenue is filled with symbols of road and railroad history, while the Santa Fe freight house is the sole original reminder of the Alvarado complex. Farther west, the 1937-built El Vado Motel stands at the crossroads between survival and oblivion. Purchased by a developer for its strategic location, the motor court was to be bulldozed in favor of condominiums, but the city stepped in and saved it.

As with any big city, preservationists endure soaring victories and crushing defeats. The Santa Fe shops and the El Vado represent the biggest and smallest examples of places that fall somewhere in between; only time will reveal their ultimate fates.

Opposite: Freight house
Above: Santa Fe shops and Central
Avenue signs

SANTA FE

At 7,000 feet, Santa Fe is America's oldest capital city and a mecca for Southwest history and Native American culture. While snubbed by the railroad that bore its name, save for an 18-mile spur, the historic city was home to Route 66 for its first eleven years. The original road into New Mexico crossed west from Texas through Tucumcari and Santa Rosa, then turned northward 59 miles to Romeroville, where it joined with U.S. 85 across Glorieta Pass. The highway navigated downtown Santa Fe and turned south to Albuquerque via Bernalillo and the Rio Grande Valley.

As Route 66 was commissioned in November 1926, Governor Arthur T. Hannett had just lost his bid for re-election. Hannett sought a direct route from Santa Rosa to Albuquerque, but Santa Fe and other northern cities bitterly fought the idea; they were instrumental in preventing his second term. Angered, he set out to have the last laugh. He mobilized a fleet of machinery and men, and gave them 31 days in December to build a 69-mile road to Moriarty, where it would connect with an existing route. Teams started work at both ends and raced to meet in the middle. By January 3, 1927, when new governor Richard C. Dillon sent his own engineer to view "Hannett's Joke," a graded road was already in service. Ten years later, it would officially become the new home of Route 66.

Santa Fe was hardly in danger of being forgotten. Seventy years later, the New Mexico capital remains a premiere destination for artists and tourists. In 1992, Santa Fe Railway sold its spur from Lamy to the Santa Fe Southern Railway, and the city gained a new tourist railroad. The popular line celebrated its fifteenth anniversary in 2007. SFSR still carries freight when necessary, making it one of America's last "mixed train" operations. The sprawling La Fonda, a former Harvey Hotel, stands in the center of downtown and continues its tradition as a fine hotel and restaurant. "Pre-1937" Route 66 signs line the original road through town, not far from the California Mission–style Santa Fe Depot on Guadalupe Street. The "City Different" appears to have had the last laugh.

Top left: Santa Fe depot
Top right: SFSR passenger coach
Above: Santa Fe Southern No. 93
Right: La Fonda Harvey House

SANTA FE / GLORIETA PASS / TUCUMCARI

About 130 years ago, men from the Santa Fe Railway and the Denver & Rio Grande Western Railroad faced each other with firearms, fighting for the right to build a railroad over the Raton and Glorieta passes to Albuquerque. Santa Fe won the battle, but today the line is obsolete and little-used by successor BNSF. Only Amtrak's Chicago-Los Angeles *Southwest Chief* trains are a daily fixture, and most of the route has been purchased by the state of New Mexico to serve commuters who choke traffic on nearby Interstate 25. The Rio Grande is gone, merged with the Southern Pacific Railroad, which was in turn absorbed by Union Pacific, BNSF's chief competitor.

So it's especially ironic to find former Rio Grande and AT&SF cabooses facing each other on a hidden spur in downtown Santa Fe, near the Santa Fe Southern depot on a summer morning. Cabooses themselves faded into history 20 years ago . . . just a drop in time for a town that was founded over 400 years ago.

Railroads, like the land they cross and the people who built them, are filled with beginnings and endings. The sight of the former Rio Grande No. 1440 is a fitting reminder that the end of our journey is near. Crossing Glorieta Pass on one of the few remaining sections of Route 66, a 1910 marker reveals the original route that started it all: the Santa Fe Trail.

After 800 miles together, the Santa Fe and Route 66 part ways at a tiny point called Romeroville, just west of Las Vegas, New Mexico. The Raton Subdivision swings north toward the southeast tip of Colorado, while the highway plunges south and meets up with "Hannett's Joke," now

Left: Cabooses at Santa Fe
Above: Marker, Glorieta Pass
Right: Blue Swallow, Tucumcari

buried under Interstate 40. At Santa Rosa, Route 66 joins a former Rock Island rail line, now owned by Union Pacific. They'll head to Texas by way of Tucumcari, home of the famed Blue Swallow Motel and its brilliant neon sign.

A variety of railroads shadow the Mother Road on its odyssey to Chicago, some familiar and some exotic. Along the way, the former Santa Fe and Route 66 will meet occasionally and exchange fleeting glances, sharing a few miles before again drifting apart. Like any good relationship, they'll ultimately reunite before journey's end, finishing the last miles together.

All good things may come to an end, but new beginnings lie around the next curve.

This page, clockwise from left:
Rotosphere, Moriarty
Blue Spruce Lodge, Gallup
AT&SF neon, Barstow

Neon Signs

Nothing is more quintessentially linked with Route 66 than neon. The streets along the road, illuminated with the vibrant colors of ruby red, emerald green, and sapphire blue, beckoned tourists with the promise of a delicious meal, a comfortable bed, or a cool swim. Visible even in daylight, people would stop and stare at neon Indians, teepees, cactus, thunderbirds, swallows, and other characters. Places with glowing names like Blue Swallow, Sun and Sand, Paradise, and Tee Pee Curios invited one to pause and experience something unique. Nothing else catches the eye like neon.

With the assistance of Route 66 historians, authors, and neon craftsmen, a panel was assembled to establish criteria and select candidates for restoration. Nine signs were selected, with funding provided by a combination of donations, including business owner and third party contributions. To date, ten neon signs have been restored along Route 66 in Gallup, Grants, Albuquerque, Moriarty, Santa Rosa, and Tucumcari, New Mexico.

While neon is a timeless element of the entire Route 66 experience, New Mexico has led the way in relighting these jewels.

— LAURA LAWRENCE

Left: Lightning, Kingman
Below: La Loma, Santa Rosa

The use of neon signs ignited with the repeal of prohibition, which created the need for eye-catching signs above bars. In the 1930s and 1940s, neon became synonymous with Art Deco design. By the 1950s, neon was inextricably linked with drive-ins, diners, and by extension, the American Dream itself. Because it required talent to bend a neon tube, creating a neon sign is an art form. Toward the end of the 1950s, as many of the old neon sign craftsmen retired, other forms of signage became popular using new plastics and fluorescent bulbs. Creating a plastic sign was cheaper and required no artistic talent. Thus began the demise of neon signs along the traveler's landscape.

As many of these fantastic relics lay in ruin, Elmo Baca, New Mexico's former State Historic Preservation Officer, envisioned a project to rekindle appreciation of vintage neon and its importance to Route 66. In 1999, the Route 66 Corridor Preservation Act was passed by Congress and money was designated for Route 66 preservation. The National Park Service was charged with administering the project and a Route 66 Corridor Preservation Office was established. When the office issued the first request for proposals for Route 66 preservation projects, Baca came forward with his bold idea to restore neon signs; after a competitive bidding process, the New Mexico Route 66 Association was selected to execute the project.

The Midwest

Everything changes past Santa Rosa, New Mexico. Open rangeland envelops Route 66, and the Union Pacific Railroad swings alongside the highway. It's the first of many rail lines that the road will encounter through the Midwest states to its eastern terminus in Chicago. They include consolidated giants born during the "mega-merger" era—UP, Norfolk Southern, Canadian National, and BNSF— as well as the smaller but formidable Kansas City Southern, plus regional and shortline railroads.

After eastern New Mexico and the Texas panhandle, flat rangeland eventually gives way to woods, rivers, and fields, interrupted only by a string of small towns and the big cities of Amarillo, Oklahoma City, Tulsa, St. Louis, and Chicago. As with the Southwest states, devoted people from both the towns and cities play a vital role in preserving Route 66, stubbornly keeping the road's tradition alive. Drive-in theaters, colorful motor courts, and friendly cafes await the traveler, as do reptile farms and a myriad of giant roadside creatures.

Opposite: UP special, Mazonia, Illinois
Below left: Carthage, Missouri
Below right: Truck logo, McLean, Texas

Many of the railroads that followed Route 66 through the Midwest are now just memories thanks to merger or abandonment, including the Chicago, Rock Island & Pacific, Missouri-Kansas-Texas, Alton Railroad, St. Louis-San Francisco, and the Gulf, Mobile & Ohio. Their memories survive in museums and depots, and in the occasional special train that relives a time when railroads and highways offered glamorous adventure. A perfect example is seen in 1997 at Mazonia, Illinois, as a Union Pacific business train with vintage E9 passenger diesels roars past the "half arch" bridge on alternate Route 66. The bridge was dismantled in 2001; Illinois' Department of Transportation had offered the span to anyone willing to remove it, but found no takers.

Above: Rock Island diesels, Amarillo, Texas
Right: SP 8038 at Tucumcari, NM

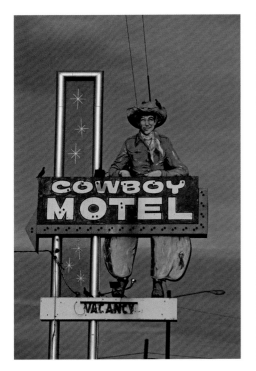

TEXAS

East of Albuquerque, Route 66 met up with the "Golden State Route" in Santa Rosa, where the Southern Pacific connected with the Rock Island's mainline to Tucumcari and points east. One of the Midwest's weaker railroads, the Rock Island entered its third and final bankruptcy in 1975, following a failed merger attempt by Union Pacific. The ailing company ran its last train in 1980. Like a vulture, Southern Pacific descended on the bones and picked up the Golden State Route. Ironically, UP finally obtained a piece of the Rock when it absorbed the SP in 1996. Nearly a year after the merger, No. 8038 waits for a crew change by the Tucumcari depot, a lone yellow diesel the only visible sign of assimilation.

Texas, the largest of the contiguous 48 states, contains the second-shortest stretch of Route 66. About 150 miles can still be driven across the flat Texas panhandle, shadowed by the remains of the "Choctaw Route," a second Rock Island line to Tucumcari. In Amarillo, a host of railroads once converged on the city, including the Rock, Missouri-Kansas-Texas, Fort Worth & Denver, and the Santa Fe. Today BNSF and UP handle most of the rail action, but Amarillo still has plenty of quirky attractions, including the "Big Texan" restaurant, home of the free 72-ounce steak (if devoured in an hour). Farther east are the small Texas towns of McLean and Shamrock, followed by the Oklahoma state line.

Above left: Amarillo, Texas
Above right: The 1936-built U-Drop Inn Cafe,
  Shamrock, Texas
Left: A Warbonnet E8 idles at Santa Fe's
  Amarillo depot in 1965

OKLAHOMA

John Steinbeck's mythical Joad family pulled up stakes and abandoned their home near Sallisaw, Oklahoma, meeting up with Route 66 in Oklahoma City for a journey that would place the Mother Road in the American consciousness. Today, nearly all the old road has been preserved and is still drivable in the state that humorist Will Rogers once called home.

The discarded Choctaw Route follows Route 66 through western Oklahoma, where the road threaded a web of familiar railroads, including the Missouri-Kansas-Texas, the Santa Fe, the Kansas City Southern, and the St. Louis-San Francisco (commonly known as "The Frisco"). The latter railroad was the highway's chief companion through eastern Oklahoma, a tiny corner of Kansas, and across Missouri.

As in other states, roadside creations and colorful creatures await the Route 66 traveler. In Catoosa, a smiling, "life size" blue whale guards a former swimming hole, and Totem Pole Park in Foyil lies under the shadow of a 90-foot totem. Spectacular bridges are a hallmark of the Midwest; near-twin structures carry Route 66 across the Verdigris River near Catoosa. The left span was built in 1936, while the right opened in 1957. Towering in the distance is the former Frisco bridge, now owned by BNSF. Realigned as part of the McClellan-Kerr River Navigation System, the Verdigris hosts ships from the Gulf of Mexico to Catoosa, the largest inland port in the U.S.

Left: Bridges near Catoosa, Oklahoma.
Right: Crossing under the old Rock
 Island line, Hydro, Oklahoma

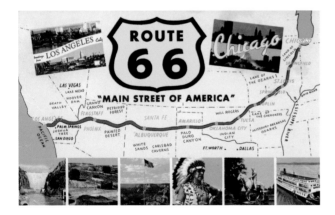

Top: Blue Whale, Catoosa, Oklahoma
Above: Main Street postcard
Right: Galloway's Totem Pole Park, Foyil, Oklahoma

KANSAS / MISSOURI

With a mere 13 miles of Mother Road pavement, Kansas is the sole Route 66 state where the replacement interstate not only bypassed the old highway, but all of its accompanying towns. On the bright side, it's possible to drive 66 across the state's southeast corner without ever encountering the superslab.

In its early decades, the road flirted briefly with "Miss Katy," the Missouri-Kansas-Texas railroad, beginning with its predecessor, the Kansas, Oklahoma & Gulf. Road and railroad crossed in Baxter Springs and in Galena, where 66 passed the MKT passenger depot. Today the former station is a museum complete with switch engine, caboose,

Above: Galena station, Kansas

and relics that highlight the history of this mining region. Near Baxter Springs, the March Arch Bridge is only one of three such historic structures to be preserved in the Sunflower State.

Crossing into Missouri, the former Frisco railroad loosely follows Route 66 through the forested limestone hills of the Ozarks, interrupted only by small towns such as Joplin, Carthage, and Springfield. The road spans over 300 miles of the Show Me State; unspoiled farmland and pastoral views dominate as the old road angles north to St. Louis. A variety of railroad companies once called on the city, and contemporary rainbows still materialize—such as the colorful trio of diesels from Kansas City Southern, Gateway Western, and Texas Mexican, rolling past the St. Louis Gateway Arch and the city's skyline in 1997.

Right: Kansas arch bridge
Opposite: St. Louis Arch

MISSOURI / ILLINOIS

The character of Route 66 across Missouri consists largely of the four-lane variety. Much of the old road was upgraded and expanded during the 1950s, and some sections were rebuilt to standards matching nearby Interstate 44. In 2006, four lanes of 66 pass under a BNSF freight in St. Louis on the old Frisco mainline from Springfield. Twenty-six years after a 1980 merger with the Burlington Northern, the bridge boldly urges drivers to "Ship it on the Frisco."

Across the Mississippi River from St. Louis, Route 66 enters the final state of its eastbound journey—Illinois, the land of Lincoln. The road once encountered a dizzying number of rail companies in this state, including the Chicago, Burlington & Quincy, the Wabash, the Baltimore & Ohio, and the Alton. The Illinois Central closely paralleled 66 through wooded hills and the towns of Staunton, Litchfield, and Springfield, President Lincoln's hometown.

Below: BNSF and Frisco bridge, St. Louis

Far left: Hamel, Illinois
Left: Pig Hip sign
Below: ICG, Dwight, Illinois

North of Springfield, the Alton Railroad became Route 66's companion for the final miles to Chicago, although it would later become the "Alton Route" of the Gulf, Mobile & Ohio Railroad.

Although GM&O and its predecessors were noted for excellent Chicago–St. Louis passenger service on the line beside Route 66, freight traffic could never compete with nearby Santa Fe's direct route from Chicago to Kansas City and the west. GM&O would eventually merge with the Illinois Central to become the Illinois Central Gulf; today the mainline is part of the Union Pacific empire.

While trains keep Route 66 travelers company, roadside attractions are equally plentiful. A restored barn near Hamel, Illinois, points westbound drivers to Missouri's Meramec Caverns, while the Pig Hip restaurant in Broadwell served its namesake sandwiches until owner Ernie Edwards converted it into a museum. Sadly, an electrical fire claimed the museum in 2007, another Route 66 icon lost.

Decades ago, cabooses vanished into history, but in 1975 they still rolled beside the Mother Road in Illinois. Seen near Dwight, a rare ex-Pennsylvania Railroad car brings up the rear of a northbound Illinois Central Gulf freight.

Left: IC train with Chicago skyline
Right: Metra at Joliet, Illinois
Below: GM&O train near Bloomington

ILLINOIS

In the Gulf, Mobile & Ohio era, four F-unit diesels are in charge of freight No. 32 as it approaches Bloomington, Illinois, on an August 1963 morning. The four-lane U.S. 66 is visible at left; today Interstate 55 is close to this alignment, with the two-lane southbound pavement surviving as a local road. North of Bloomington is Plainfield, where a brief section of Route 66 shared signage with another famous road—U.S. 30, the Lincoln Highway.

In the 1930s, Route 66 was rerouted to Plainfield by way of a new alignment, and the original highway through Joliet became an alternate. The Santa Fe reunites with 66 as both enter the outskirts of Chicago; the city has long been the country's railroad capital, and even today the big rail companies all have a presence: BNSF, Union Pacific, Norfolk Southern, Illinois Central (now part of Canadian National), Canadian Pacific, CSX Transportation, Amtrak, and smaller regional lines. The area's commuter agency, Metra, also joins the action with a fleet of colorful trains, such as one seen near a cluster of highway signs in Joliet.

And suddenly, finally, we've arrived in Chicago. Miles of Route 66 continue through the city, under "El" trains and through downtown's steel and glass canyons. The eastern terminus was originally at the intersection of Michigan Avenue and Jackson Boulevard, but it was extended in 1937 to East Jackson and Lake Shore Drive. The final mile of the eight-state journey ends in view of the Santa Fe Railway's former corporate headquarters at 80 East Jackson. The historic building still sports a tall "Santa Fe" sign on its roof—a harbinger of the close relationship these two routes share through the American Southwest.

The Santa Fe building is lost amid the skyline of the Windy City, which frames an Illinois Central train leaving town in 1998. It's a fitting finale to nearly 300 miles of Illinois driving, and to our cross-country odyssey via the Mother Road.

The Ghost of Tom Joad

"66 is the mother road, the road of flight."
— JOHN STEINBECK, *The Grapes of Wrath*

Like Steinbeck's Joad family, the Dust Bowl refugees of the 1930s first gazed at the promised land of California from Topock, Arizona, looking across the mighty Colorado River. That view revealed a forbidding desert seemingly without end. Despite overcoming all manner of hardships—oppressive weather, the scorn of fellow Americans—this bleak panorama was what finally snapped their spirits. Some turned their rigs around and headed east without even a backward glance. Others pushed forward across the Mojave with grim intent; those with financial means paid to have their vehicles moved west on Santa Fe flatcars. Many crossed the Mojave after sunset, using the cover of darkness to escape the scorching heat.

Driving Route 66 at night strips away the trappings of time and progress, and restores the old Santa Fe and its asphalt companion to their basic elements. As the headlights of modern diesels rush through the gathering darkness, pacing scattered cars and trucks on the road, it's hard not to imagine the days when travel wasn't so comfortable and sanitized. Imagine the sinking realization of a stranded Dust Bowl family on the highway shoulder, watching the lights of a *Super Chief* roar past . . . dreams shattered by something as random as a shredded fanbelt.

Sadly, broken dreams are part of the Mother Road experience. But so are the glory days that the road and railroad enjoyed for decades. Legacies of boom and bust endure: a rusted Ford in Mesita, New Mexico, recalls the great migration past mesas and motor courts, bound for the promised land of California. As night falls on the Mojave, ghostly double-sixes point the way to adventure beyond the former Santa Fe rails. And in the quiet moments before sunrise, the stillness of the Colorado River is shattered by the passage of a westbound Santa Fe train. The following pages celebrate the moods and mysteries of the Route 66 Railway.

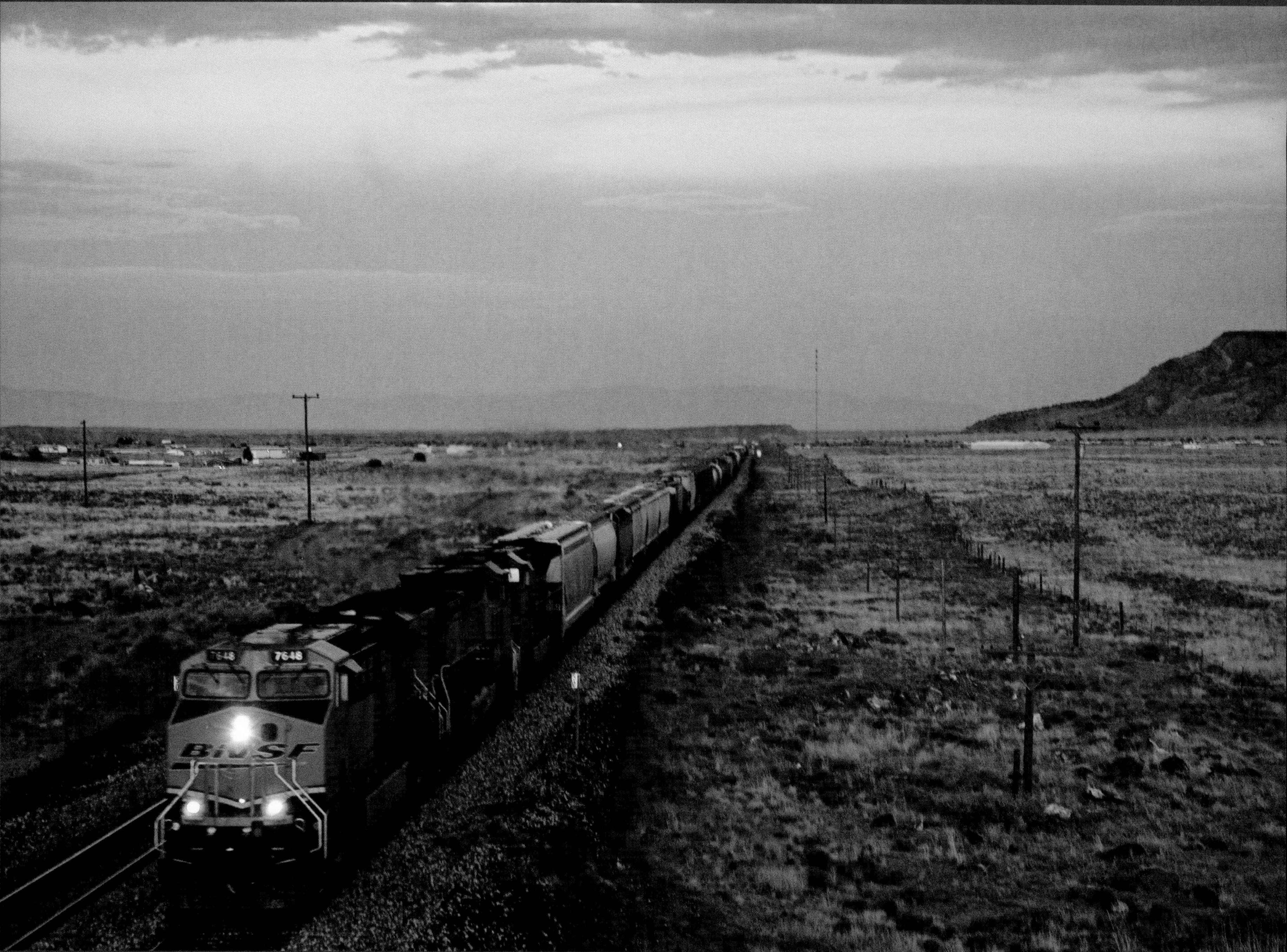
7648
7648
BNSF

Wide open spaces follow the road and railroad from California to New Mexico, bringing isolation and calm to those seeking refuge from the hurried pace of an overdeveloped West. At sunset, waves of dust stream between the rails of the BNSF mainline and Route 66 near Seligman, Arizona. Few outpost towns remain in the California desert, some reduced to clusters of railroad signals and road signs—such as those that crowd below a menacing cantilever structure at Goffs, California. And in Correo, New Mexico, the passage of a westbound train at dusk seems small and insignificant under panoramic clouds in the western sky.

The Dust Bowl decimated the fortunes of farmers in the Midwest, sending them and their families onto Route 66 in search of a better life. But such storms aren't confined to the Midwest states; Arizona's summer monsoon season can trigger blinding dust storms with frightening regularity.

One such tempest batters northern Arizona during an August afternoon, as winds whip across the Toltec Divide. Visibility has dropped to near-zero for drivers on Interstate 40, but the railroad keeps rolling. Viewed from the Coppertown Road overpass in Winslow, a BNSF freight heads west toward Flagstaff. As it navigates the undulating terrain, the headlight of an eastbound appears on the horizon. Within moments the westbound's rear engines are consumed by a wall of sand that blurs the San Francisco Peaks, and pursues the oncoming train. The photographer snaps a final frame and leaps inside his truck, but the wave crests before reaching town. It's still a harrowing sight that reminds onlookers of nature's raw power. Driving to Flagstaff, it's hard not to wonder how Dust Bowl families coped as they crossed the Southwest in their rickety vehicles.

Splashes of light and color brighten the California desert after the sun sinks behind the horizon. In the Mojave, more motorists than residents note the passing of a Union Pacific freight through tiny Daggett, while an emerald motel sign in Barstow silently beckons Route 66 travelers. East of Ludlow, the slow descent of crossing gates resembles an extraterrestrial encounter, thanks to the eerie glow cast by an adjacent signal. A few miles west, the diesels of a Santa Fe eastbound appear to spurn all color, leaving the ghosts of the Tonopah & Tidewater behind in a monochrome scene.

Get Your Kicks on Route 66 . . . Santa Fe All the Way. These slogans have echoed through decades of change. The icons they represent are no more and yet they loom larger than ever, fueled by nostalgia and a search for identity. The sight of a modern Corvette at Amboy, halted by a passing BNSF train, and a 1950-built dome car in Arizona's Kaibab Forest illustrate the revival of road and railroad, more than 80 years after they were joined.

What, then, is the mystical connection between these paths of steel and asphalt?

They share dreams. Over a century ago, those dreams lived in the hearts of railroad men who looked west from Albuquerque toward the Arizona Divide and a new way of life. Eighty years ago, they captured the hearts of motorists who braved the adventure of a lifetime. Thirty years ago, those dreams seemed broken, as train stations and motor courts alike collapsed in the wake of the interstate.

But today the dreams are restored, as BNSF trains roll like streetcars past wigwam motels and Harvey Houses. They're alive in the sparkling eyes of Angel Delgadillo as another tour bus rumbles to a stop on a warm summer's day. Once again, the legends of Route 66 and the Santa Fe Railway color the towns of the American Southwest. Children still gaze out of the family car and wave to a passing train, wondering what surprises lie around the next curve. More than 20 years after the last segment of U.S. Highway 66 was bypassed through Williams, Arizona, over 80 percent of the entire road can still be driven. Once-forgotten towns again hum with life.

Looking down on downtown Flagstaff on a cold November evening, the bustling flow of Route 66 traffic and a westbound BNSF train creates a symphony of light. The dreams of Holliday and Avery are alive and well.

INDEX

SELECTED RESOURCES

Books and Articles

Armstrong, William Patrick. *Fred Harvey: Creator of Western Hospitality*. Canyonlands Publications, 2000.

Blaszak, Michael W. "Santa Fe: A Chronology." *Pacific RailNews*, No. 384 (November 1995), Pentrex, Inc.

McClanahan, Jerry. *The EZ66 Guide for Travelers*. National Historic Route 66 Federation, 2005.

Myrick, David F. *Railroads of Nevada and Eastern California, Volume 2* (reprinted). University of Nevada Press, 1992.

Myrick, David F. *The Santa Fe Route: Railroads of Arizona, Volume 4*. Signature Press, 1998.

Palmer, Mo. *Albuquerque Then and Now*. Thunder Bay Press, 2006.

Poling-Kempes, Lesley. *The Harvey Girls: Women Who Opened the West*. Paragon House, 1989.

Snyder, Tom. *The Route 66 Traveler's Guide and Roadside Companion*. St. Martin's Press, 1990.

Steinbeck, John. *The Grapes of Wrath*. Penguin Books, 1939.

Steinheimer, Richard. "Mojave Crossing." *Trains* Magazine, Vol. 37, No. 10 (August 1977), Kalmbach Publishing Co.

Strein, Robert, John Vaughan, and C. Fenton Richards, Jr. *Santa Fe The Chief Way*. New Mexico Magazine, 2001.

Wallis, Michael. *Route 66: The Mother Road*. St. Martin's Press, 1990.

Walker, Chard L. Cajon: *Rail Passage to the Pacific*. Trans-Anglo Books, 1985.

Web Sites

Altamont Press Publishing, www.altamontpress.com

California Route 66 Preservation Foundation, www.cart66pf.org

Historic Route 66 Association of Arizona, www.azrt66.com

Los Angeles Railroad Heritage Foundation, www.larhf.org

National Historic Route 66 Federation, www.national66.com

New Mexico Route 66 Association, www.rt66nm.org

Route 66 Magazine, www.route66magazine.com

San Bernardino Railroad Historical Society, www.sbrhs.org

Santa Fe Railway Historical & Modeling Society, www.atsfrr.com

Trains **Magazine**, www.trainsmag.com

Visit the **Route 66 Railway** *book site at www.66rails.com.*

The author, Barstow, California, 1972. *Charles Lawrence*

All photographs © 2008 by Elrond Lawrence except for the following:

pgs. 8-11: all Ted Benson
p. 14: Howard Ande
p. 15: Gordon Glattenberg
p. 16: left, Stan Kistler collection; right, H. J. Prior, Stan Kistler collection
p. 18: Northern Arizona University, Cline Library, Special Collections and Archives, H.A. Clark Collection
p. 19: top, H. J. Prior, Stan Kistler collection; bottom, courtesy *Route 66 Magazine*
p. 20: Edward Kemp, courtesy Palace of the Governors (MNM/DCA)
p. 21: top, Northern Arizona University, Cline Library, Special Collections and Archives
p. 22: Center for Southwest Research, University Libraries, University of New Mexico
p. 23: Stan Kistler
pgs. 24-27: all Gordon Glattenberg
p. 28: both Hank Graham
p. 29: top, Bob Finan
pgs. 30-31: all Gordon Glattenberg
p. 32: Tom Gildersleeve
p. 33: bottom left and right, Gordon Glattenberg
p. 45: Bob Finan
p. 46: bottom right, Richard Sugg
p. 52: John Sistrunk
p. 56: Greg McDonnell
p. 91: bottom right, Hank Graham
p. 114: bottom, Kathryn Lawrence
p. 124: top, Bob Finan
p. 129: John Sistrunk
p. 130: bottom, Howard Ande
p. 144: top right, John Sistrunk
p. 145: top, Howard Ande
p. 146: left, John Sistrunk; right, Howard Ande
p. 147: Howard Ande
p. 148: top, David Lustig; bottom, Howard Ande
p. 149: top left and right, Howard Ande; bottom, Gordon Glattenberg
pgs. 150-151: both John Sistrunk
p. 152: top and right, Howard Ande
p. 153: John Sistrunk
pgs. 154-155: both Howard Ande
p. 156: John Sistrunk
p. 157: top left, John Sistrunk; top right, Howard Ande; bottom, J. David Ingles
p. 158: Howard Ande
p. 159: top, John Sistrunk; bottom, J. David Ingles
p. 164: Kathryn Lawrence

Endpaper maps by David Styffe
Postcards, pgs. 21, 34, 42, 80, 118, 137, 152: John Sistrunk collection
A&P memos, p. 17: Mike Martin collection
Out West ads, pgs. 17, 34; Rod's menus, p. 103: Elrond Lawrence collection

ISBN: 978-0-615-21407-8
Text copyright © 2008 by Elrond Lawrence
Published by the Los Angeles Railway Heritage Foundation
Design by SchoeneHauser Design
Printed in Singapore by Tien Wah Press

Los Angeles Railroad Heritage Foundation
1500 West Alhambra Road
Alhambra, California 91801

www.larhf.org

Page 1: Goffs Cultural Center, California

Page 2: BNSF and Wigwam Motel, Holbrook, Arizona

Page 4: Auxiliary tender logo, Williams, Arizona

Page 5: Signal box near Ludlow, California

Library of Congress Cataloging-in-Publication Data

Lawrence, Elrond G., 1966-
 Route 66 railway : the story of Route 66 and the Santa Fe Railway in the American Southwest / Elrond Lawrence. — First American Edition
    p. cm.
 Includes bibliographical references and index.
 ISBN 978-0-615-21407-8 (hardcover)
1. United States Highway 66—History. 2. Atchison, Topeka, and Santa Fe Railroad Company—History. 3. Roads—Southwest, New—History. 4. Automobile travel—Southwest, New—History. 5. Railroads—Southwest, New—History. 6. Railroad travel—Southwest, New—History. 7. Southwest, New—History, Local. 8. Southwest, New—History, Local—Pictorial works. 9. United States Highway 66—Pictorial works. 10. Atchison, Topeka, and Santa Fe Railroad Company—Pictorial works. I. Title.

HE356.U55L39 2008
385.0979—dc22

2008029210